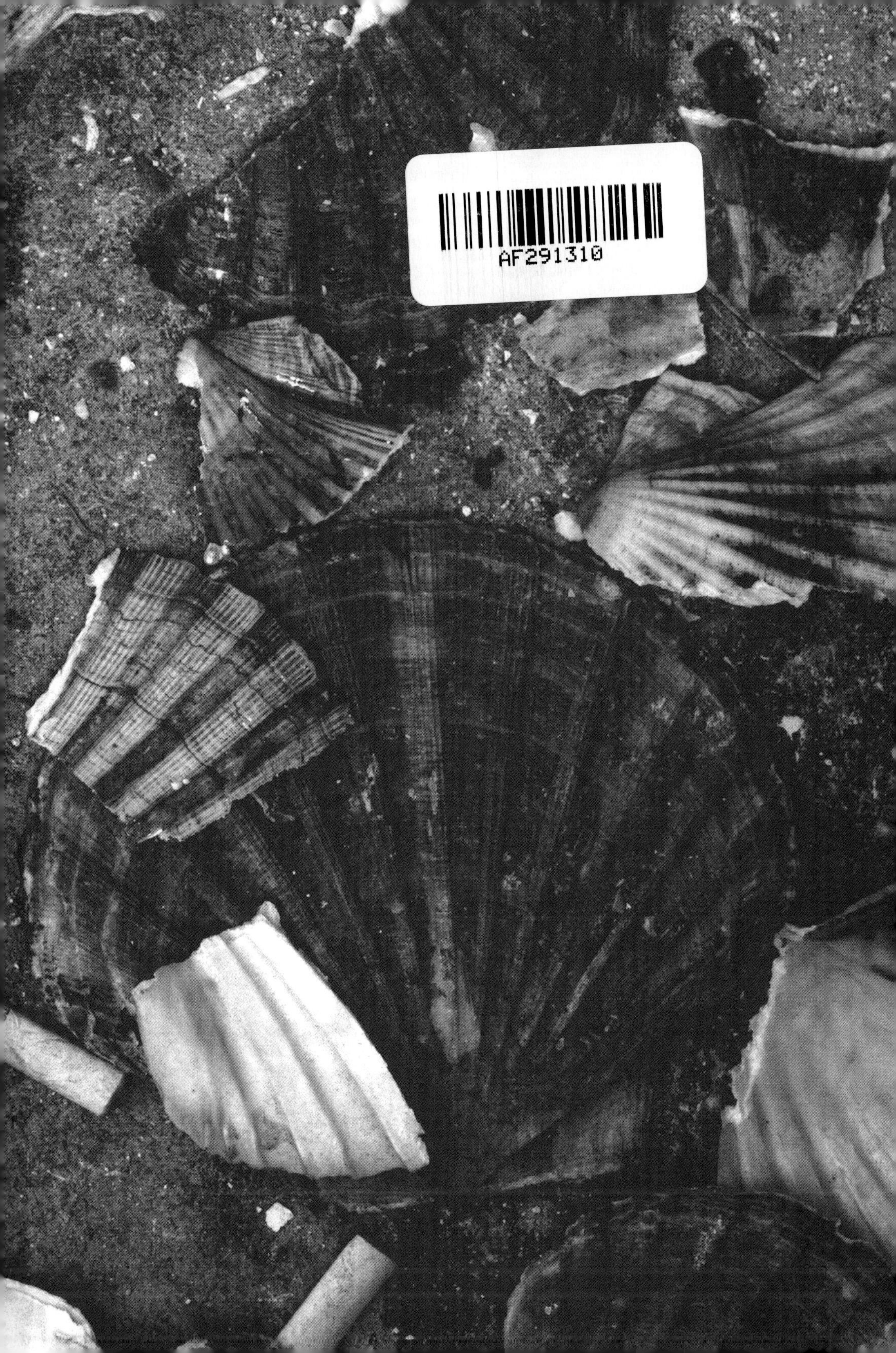

AF291310

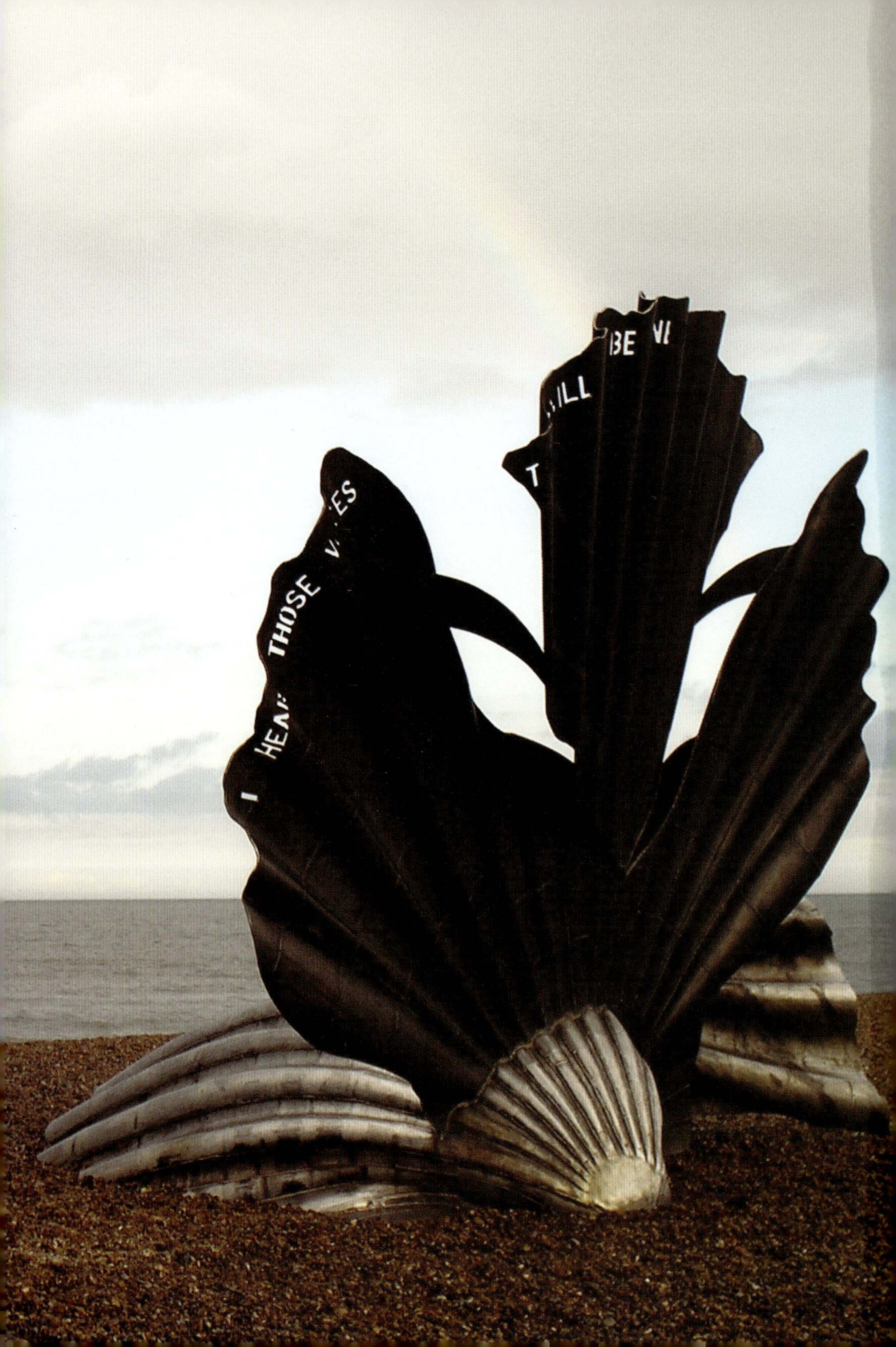
THOSE V ES
I HEA
ILL
BE N
T

THE ALDEBURGH
SCALLOP

THE ALDEBURGH
SCALLOP

MAGGI HAMBLING

FOREWORD BY
STEPHEN FRY

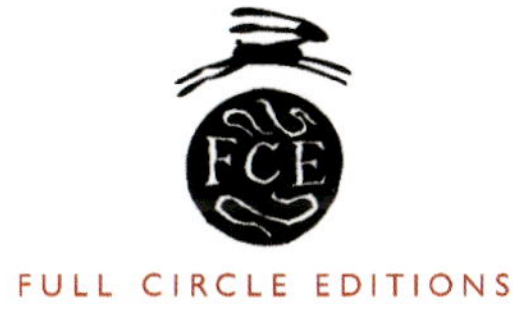

FULL CIRCLE EDITIONS

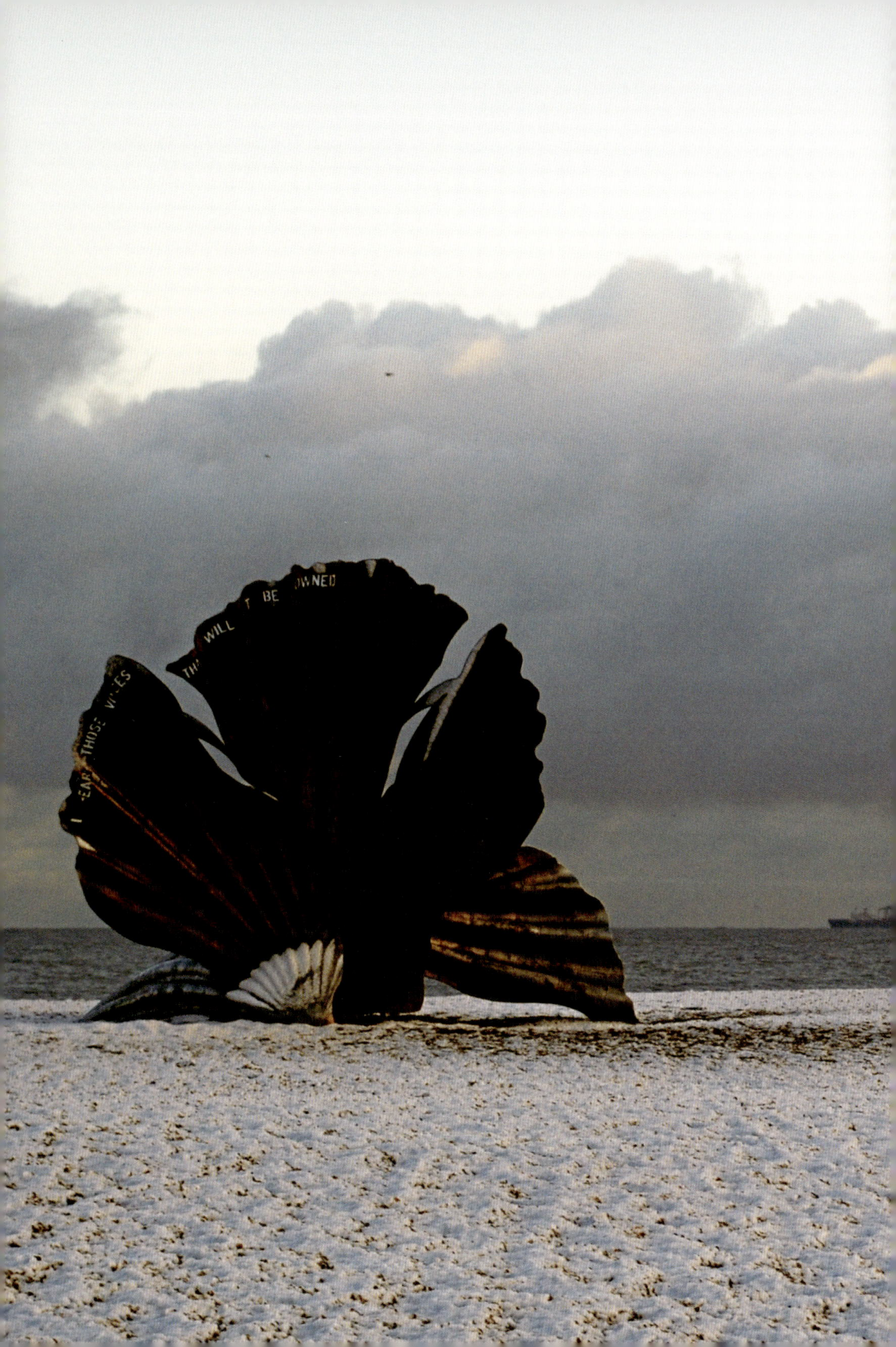
EAR THOSE VOICES
THAT WILL   T BE   OWNED

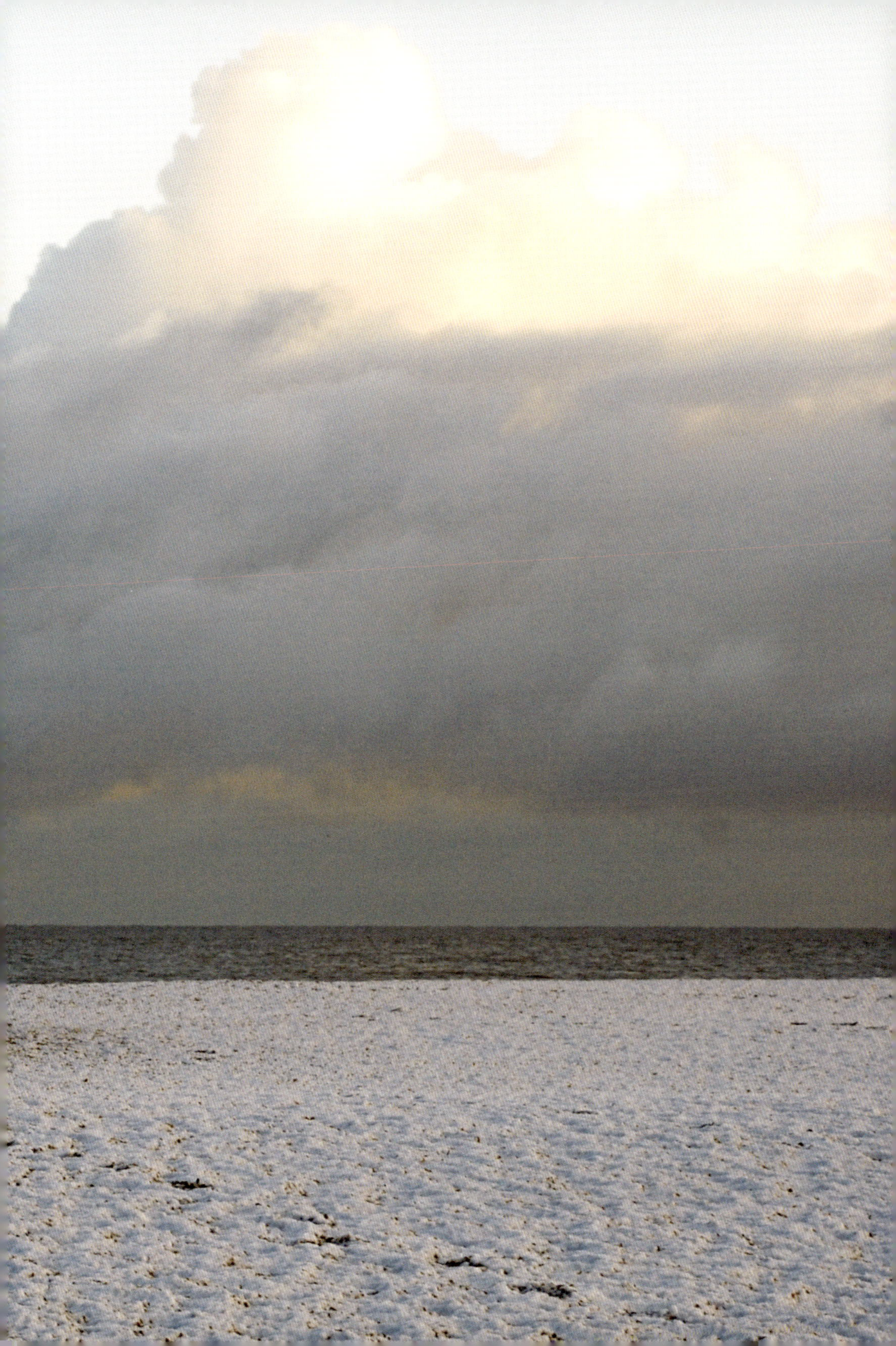

Contents

Foreword by Stephen Fry   10

Part one: the idea   15
Part two: flashback   29
Part three: fast forward   43

You are the sea   61

Other voices   63

Simon Loftus 64 | Dennis Pegg 70 | Maggy Wilson 71
Jonathan Reekie 72 | Ray Herring 72 | Sam Pegg 75
Jason Gathorne-Hardy—Survey 76
Letter to the Aldeburgh Gazette 78 | Roger Hambling 79

A selection of press coverage   80
Curriculum vitae   82
Acknowledgements   84

Foreword
by Stephen Fry

I have tried very hard to understand the point of view of those who dislike Maggi Hambling's *Scallop* and I just can't get it. The object is striking and remarkable in exactly the way the Suffolk coast is striking and remarkable—in a strong, stark frightening way that becomes more and more beautiful the more times you engage with it. The first time I walked the shingle of Aldeburgh I found the town, its shoreline and louring sea frightening and bleak—the more I got used to it, the more marvellous it became, the more I needed it and the more its peculiar beauty became profounder than the more obvious prettiness of the Cotswolds or the Downs.

The two most memorable pieces of art to celebrate this extraordinary landscape are Britten's *Peter Grimes* and Maggi's *Scallop*, which of course owes much to (and quotes) the Britten masterpiece. Both are uncomfortable, both relish the harshness, the loneliness and the ineluctable cruelty of the sea, yet both win through with humanity and glory. Maggi's work has, furthermore, the inestimable advantage of being fun. Dogs and children know instantly how to enjoy and befriend it. That it is controversial is inevitable, but that it is fitting and strong and wise is certain. It is a public work to be celebrated in countless private and familial encounters. Just think what a place of memory and romance it already is for so many lovers who have kissed, flirted and giggled around it. I suspect that many who originally opposed it would now be as fiercely opposed to its removal.

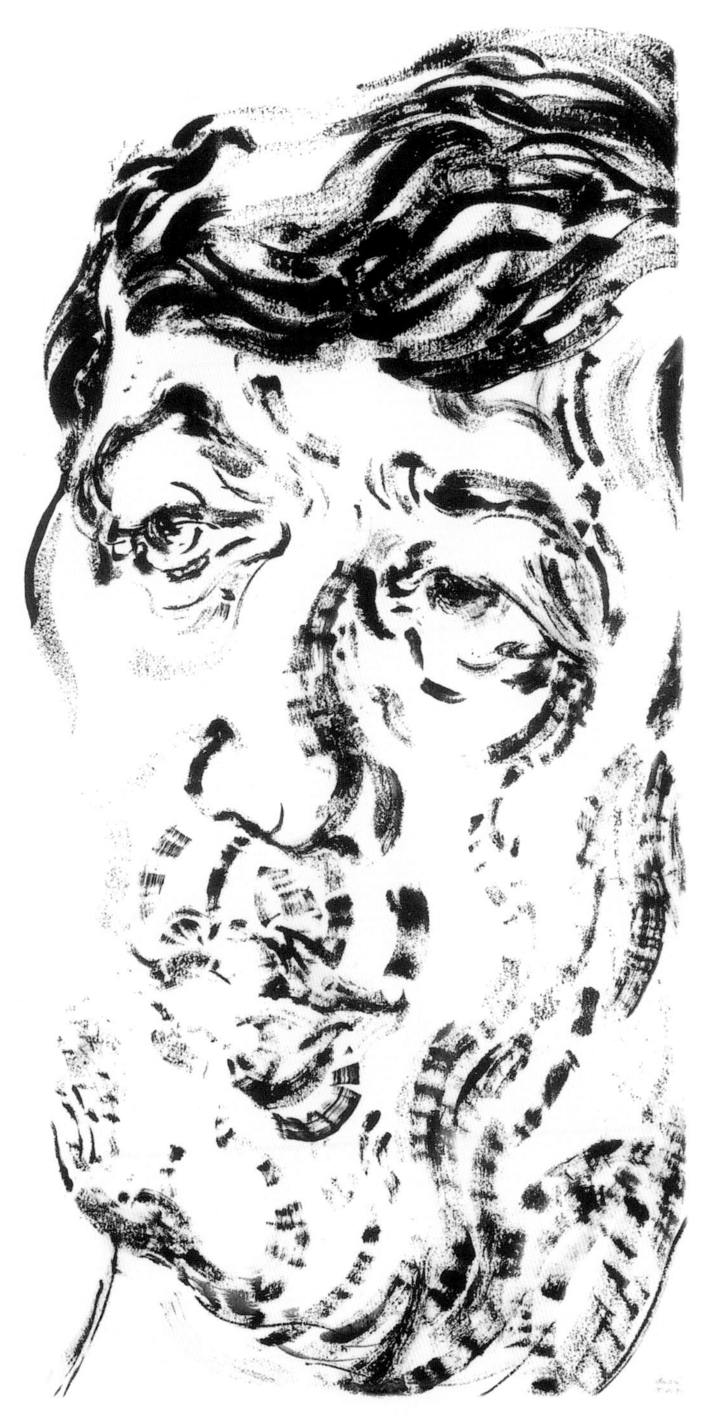

Large head of Stephen, 1993, ink on paper, 152.4 x 101.6cm

I hear those voices
that will not be drowned

from *Peter Grimes*

Right: *Scallop,* 2010, ink on paper 30 x 40cm, private collection

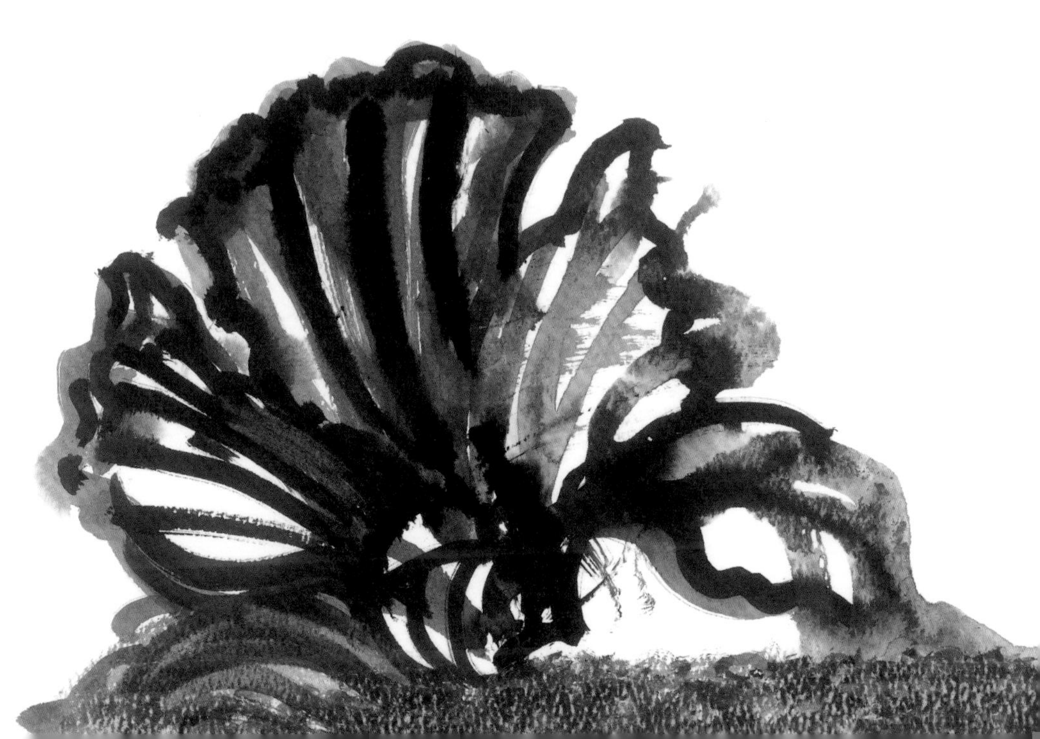

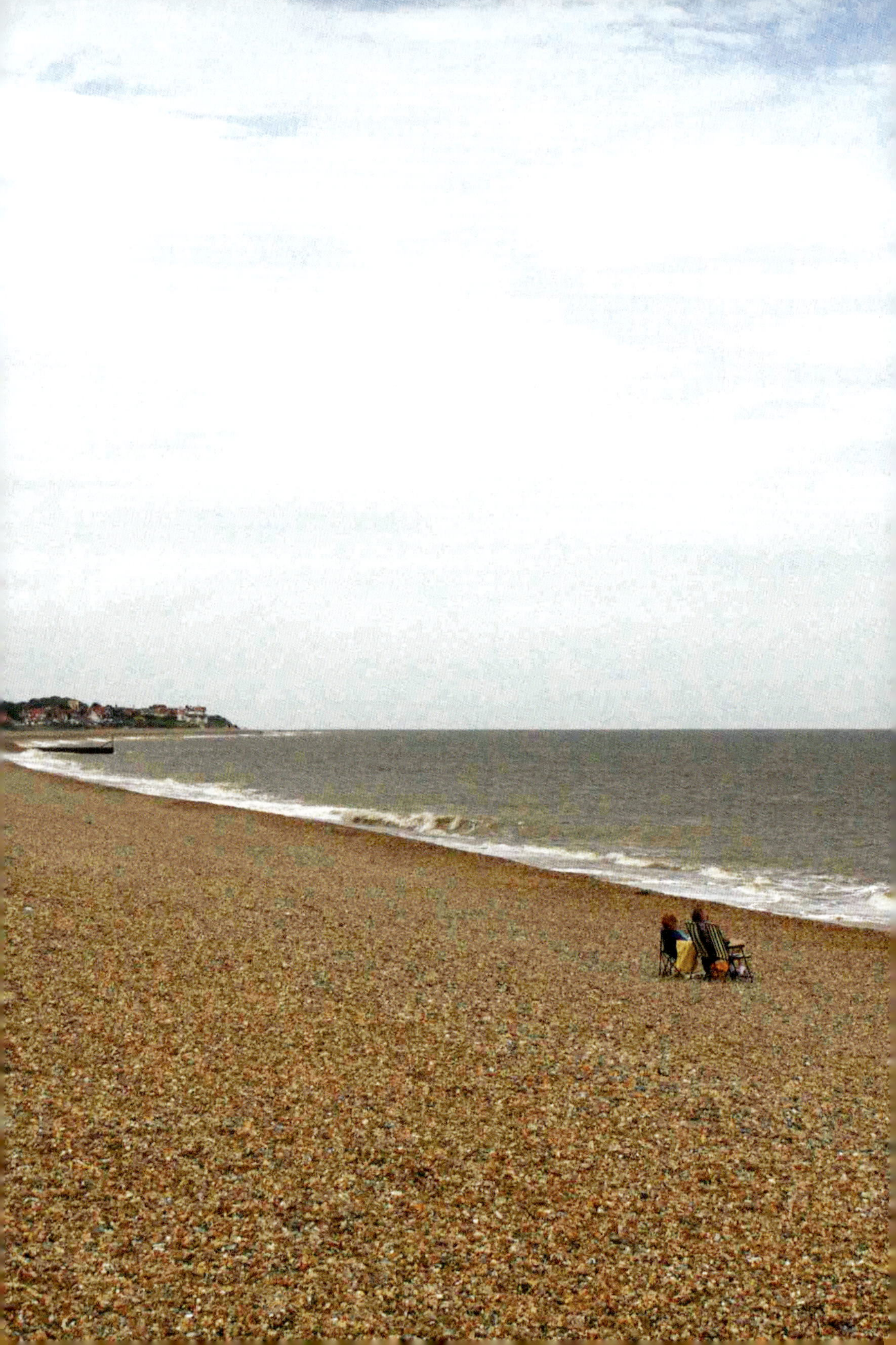

Part one: the idea

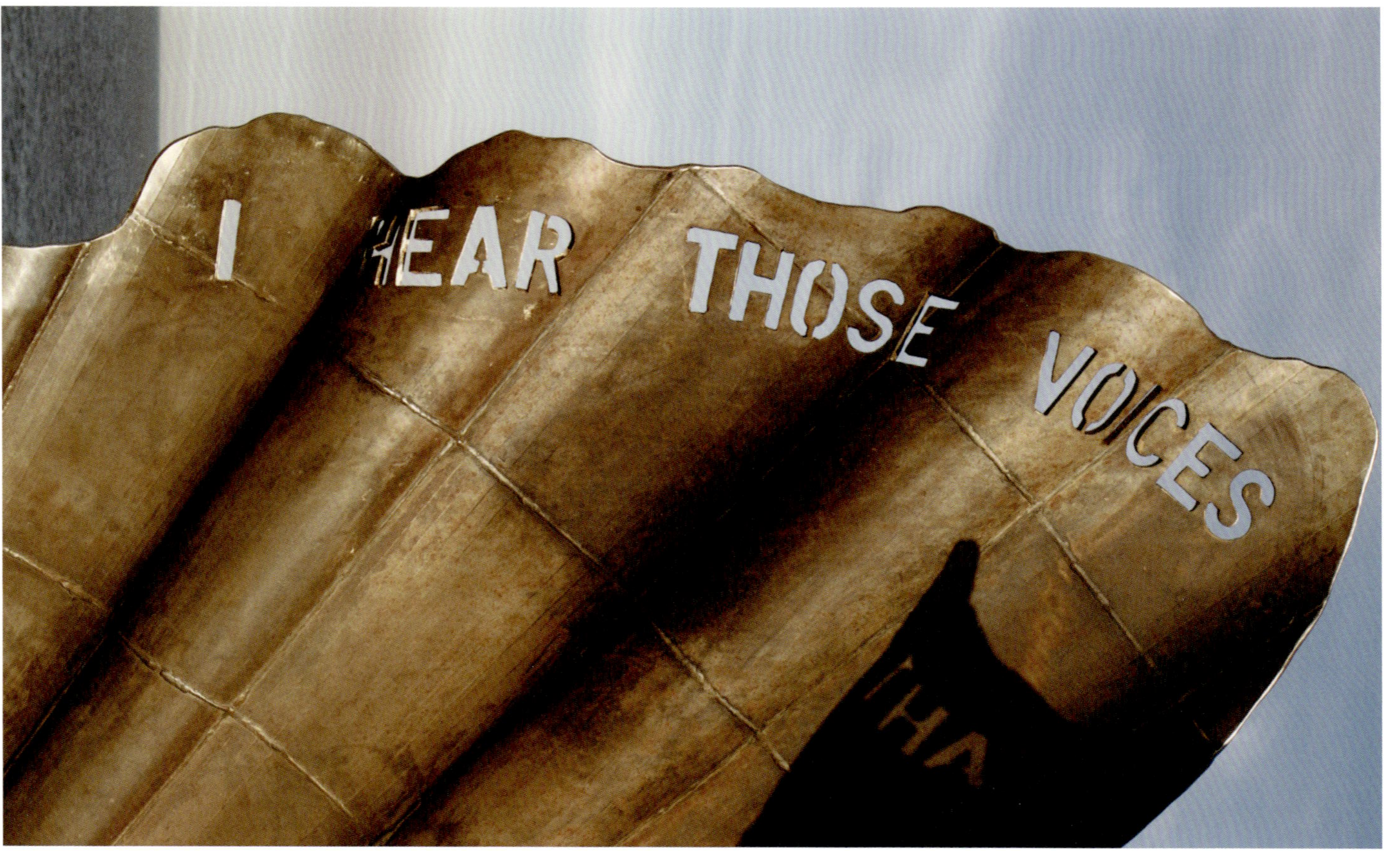
I HEAR THOSE VOICES
HA

A tall story

In the summer of 2002 a friend, the painter Vanessa Thomas, called at my cottage near the Suffolk coast. We were sitting outside having a cup of tea and in the middle of the conversation, apropos of nothing, she said, "Maggi, I've heard there's going to be a statue of Benjamin Britten in Aldeburgh and that you're going to make it."

It was the first I'd heard of it. "News to me, Vanessa," I said. "You're potty."

But later I began to think about what she'd said. I recalled newspaper reports from five years earlier saying that Aldeburgh Town Council had announced that the last thing the town wanted was a statue of Benjamin Britten. Given Britten's fame, his extraordinary music and all that he had given Aldeburgh, these newspaper reports had made me cross. I'd been deeply affected by his music. I first heard *Billy Budd*, and then *War Requiem*. They had a similar effect on me to that of hearing Oscar Wilde's stories read to us as children at school. Both Wilde's prose and Britten's music seemed to come from another place.

Two days later I decided that I would indeed like to try to create some kind of tribute to Benjamin Britten. The idea came very quickly, the idea of a shell. It came from childhood memories of holding shells to my ear to hear the sounds of the sea. I chose the scallop shell because it is a symbol of the sea and of pilgrimage, and the cradle of Venus. And, of course, there's that moment in *Some Like It Hot* when Tony Curtis is on the beach trying to seduce Marilyn Monroe by holding up a scallop as the logo of his family business …

I took a scallop shell, just as it was, to Sam Pegg because I'd been told that Peggs of

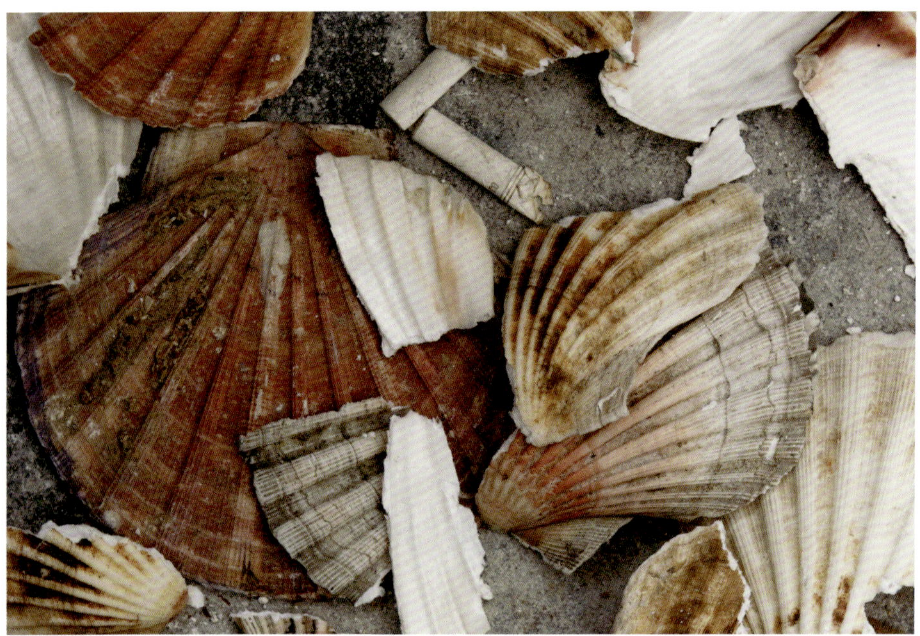

MH studio floor with smashed shells

Aldeburgh were the best steel fabricators around and I wanted my scallop to be of steel, shiny and capable of enduring the harsh environment of the Suffolk coast. Big Sam came out of his office and I handed him the scallop and said, "Could you make one of these?" He looked at it for a moment, handed it back and said, "Well, I could." Then I handed it back to him and said, "What if I wanted one of these 10 feet tall?" He handed it back to me and said eventually, "Yes, we could do it. But that big would be quite a lot of work." All the while the scallop was being handed from my small hands into Sam's big hands and back again. I said, "But would you do it?" And Sam, returning it to me, said reluctantly, "Maybe." Despite Sam's attitude I went away feeling quite optimistic that it could be done.

Topsy-turvy

My first idea was simply that of a 10ft high curved section of a scallop shell set vertically in the shingle. It would contain a seat and face the sea. I believed it would resonate with the sounds of the waves and the weather. My friend, the artist Tory Lawrence, commented that it was not very adventurous. After my initial amazement, not to say annoyance at her underwhelming response, I spent the rest of that summer experimenting with scallop shells. I made some drawings in a sketchbook but they weren't at all useful: I had to work physically with real shells, and I collected a large supply. Soon the studio floor was awash with shards of shell.

The whole scallop shell has a flat bottom and a curved top—not something I'd known before. I'd twice failed biology at school. It was somehow very important that these two elements should be reversed, so that what is naturally the bottom should be vertical and what is the top horizontal. This seemed to me to reflect Britten's work, which took classical music apart and remade it in an entirely original way, each moment composed of a new juxtaposition of sounds, like nothing I had ever heard before. The split vertical form is a metaphor for the structure of Britten's music, the split horizontal for the flow of Pears' voice, the two joined at the core of the sculpture.

So the top became the bottom and vice versa. The upper edge of the vertical shell echoes Constable's "dome of the sky", and the rising curves of steel leading to it recall the shafts of light in my Suffolk *Sunrise Paintings* of the '80s (p.41). There are

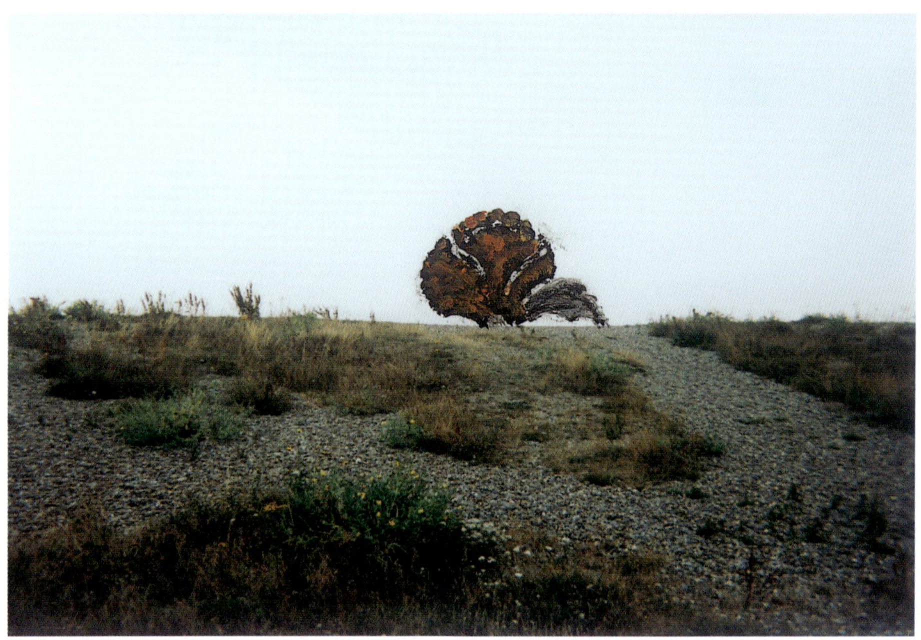

Visualisation of *Scallop,* 2002, acrylic paint on photograph

suggestions of wings of a gull in flight, the fin of a fish swimming, and the striations of the shell itself echo the undulations of the sea. I wanted it to be very much a sea piece—in much the same way as Britten's *Sea Interludes* are. And *Scallop* is subtitled *A conversation with the sea*.

So it had, of course, to be on the shingle, close to the sea. The sculpture stands on the stretch of beach that Britten walked and where I'm told he swam every day of the year. And I wanted to provide a place of contemplation where someone, whatever his or her state of mind, would be invited to contemplate the sea, the horizon, to think, as most people do when they look at the sea, about time and life and death.

I worked on the maquette. I wanted a strangeness, like the unlikely juxtapositions of Britten's music, something come upon unexpectedly as one drove along the road between Aldeburgh and Thorpeness. A shell much larger than life, and not only much larger than life but appearing to be dropped from the sky, thrown inland by the waves or forced up through the shingle. If sufficiently interested, a visitor, having crossed the shingle, discovers the explosion of the dismembered shell facing the sea.

That haunting line from *Peter Grimes*, "I hear those voices that will not be drowned", is absolutely right, an integral part of the conception of *Scallop*. The words are cut through the steel so that you read them as if they are written in the sky, whether the sun is rising or setting. I chose them also because the phrase has universal significance. We all have

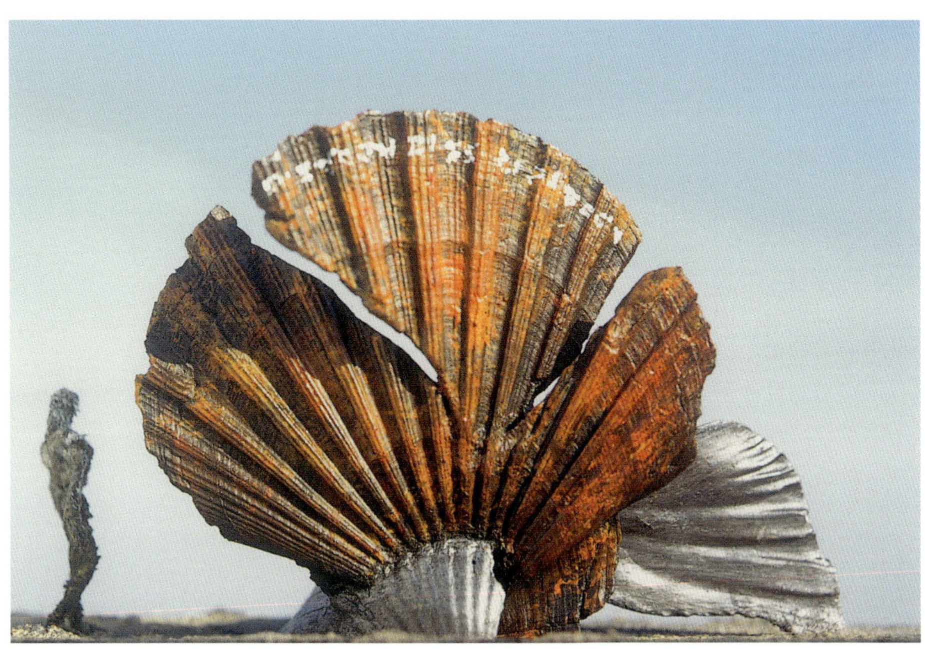

Maquette for *Scallop,* 2002, shell, sand and cardboard - view from Thorpeness Road

voices inside us all the time, whether we're awake or asleep. People are encouraged to contemplate the horizon and the movement of the waves, and to have a conversation not only with the sea but also with themselves. To listen to their own voices.

In my slow Suffolk way I realized many years later that the seed of *Scallop* was sown inside me when I was seven, watching fireworks exploding over the sea at Aldeburgh for the Coronation, or even earlier—as a toddler talking to the waves.

I worked away at the maquette, and was at last happy with it. Then came the small matter of turning it into reality. Most people think I was commissioned because most public works are commissioned. But in the case of *Scallop* that was not so. Quite the opposite. I had both to raise the money and obtain all the permissions needed to install her on that spot of beach. A long battle lay ahead.

Touch-and-go

The first person I invited to see the maquette was Jonathan Reekie, who runs Aldeburgh Music at Snape Maltings. He liked it very much, and I thought, "Wonderful. So there'll be money to make it." That was the first of many misconceptions. Of course it takes an awful lot of money to fund Aldeburgh Music, all the money Jonathan can find, and there certainly wouldn't have been any for *Scallop*.

But Jonathan thought he could put me in touch with a few people who might be helpful. I also took the maquette over to the Cranbrooks at Glemham one evening, and Caroline and Gathorne's daughter Flora suggested that I get in touch with Simon Loftus, who was then in charge of Adnams Brewery. I invited Simon to the studio, and he too was very excited when he saw the maquette and I thought, "Great! He's the Chairman of Adnams. Adnams will cough up for it." But he quickly made it clear that *Scallop* was not the kind of thing the Adnams Charity could fork out for. But he liked what he saw and said he would help to make it a reality.

The next person was Maggy Wilson. Simon and I met her one Sunday morning at the White Lion in Aldeburgh. She was a Councillor on Suffolk Coastal District Council, and when she saw the maquette she too was excited. The following year was to be European Year of Culture, and Aldeburgh was involved. And as a member of Suffolk Coastal Maggy was in touch with a lot of the people possessing the power to decide whether or not *Scallop* would happen.

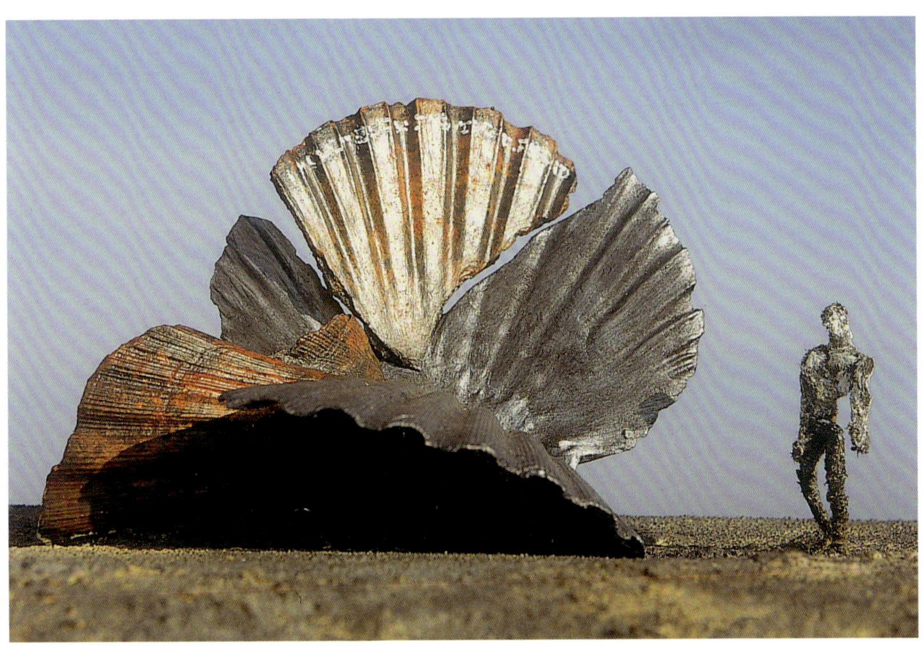

Maquette for *Scallop,* 2002, shell, sand and cardboard - view from the sea

The three of us formed an informal steering committee and took on the challenge. Letters were sent to try to drum up the finance, and Maggy began working behind the scenes to gather support for the permissions that were going to be needed if we ever managed to raise the necessary funds. The whole process took ages.

For a long time nothing much happened. I'm a naturally impatient person: once I get an idea I want to make it happen immediately. But for a long time it was touch-and-go as to whether *Scallop* would see the light of day. So for some time, and despite the encouragement of Jonathan, Simon and Maggy, I had to put *Scallop* to one side and work on other things. It was during this period that the *North Sea Paintings* began.

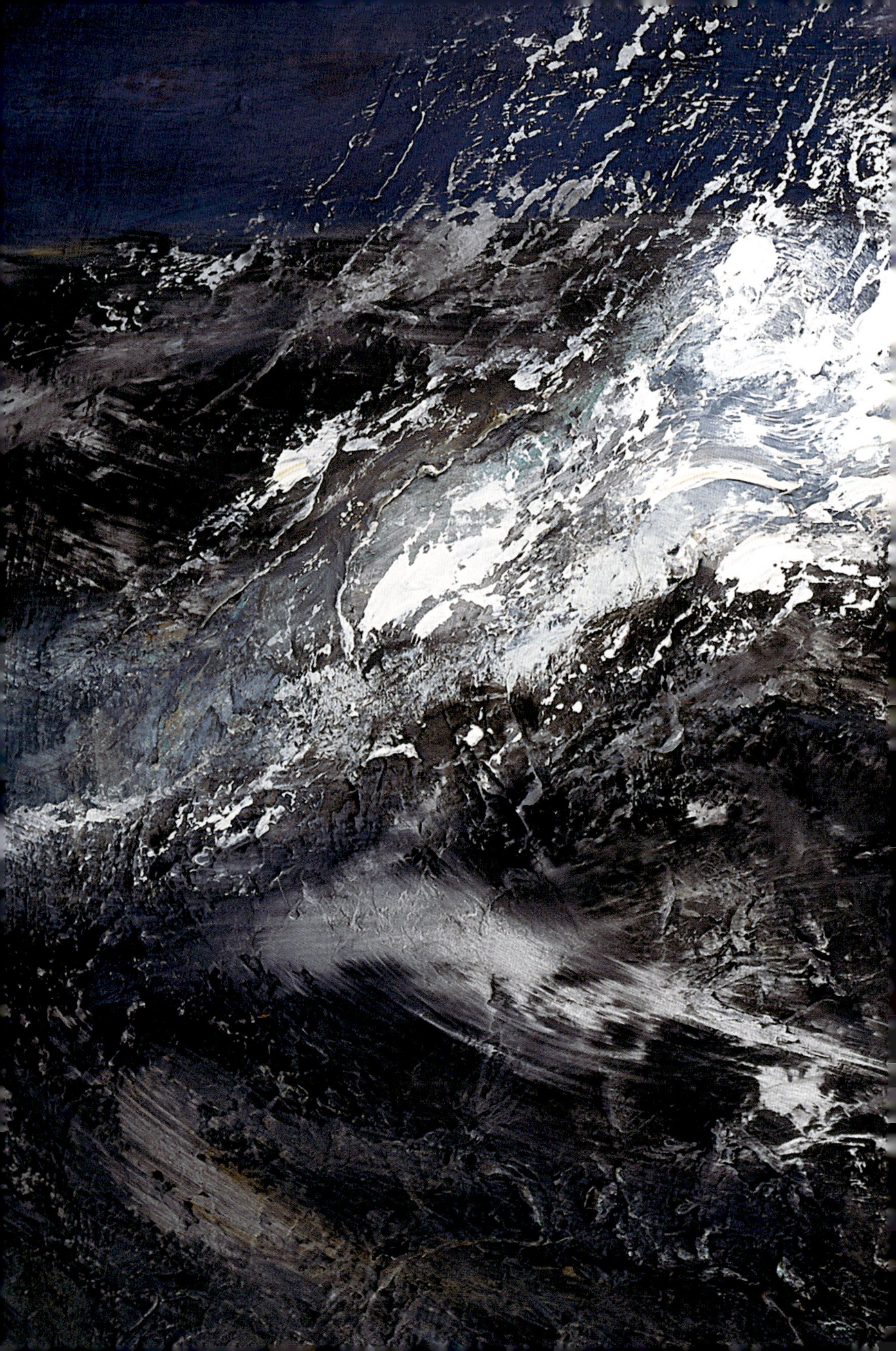

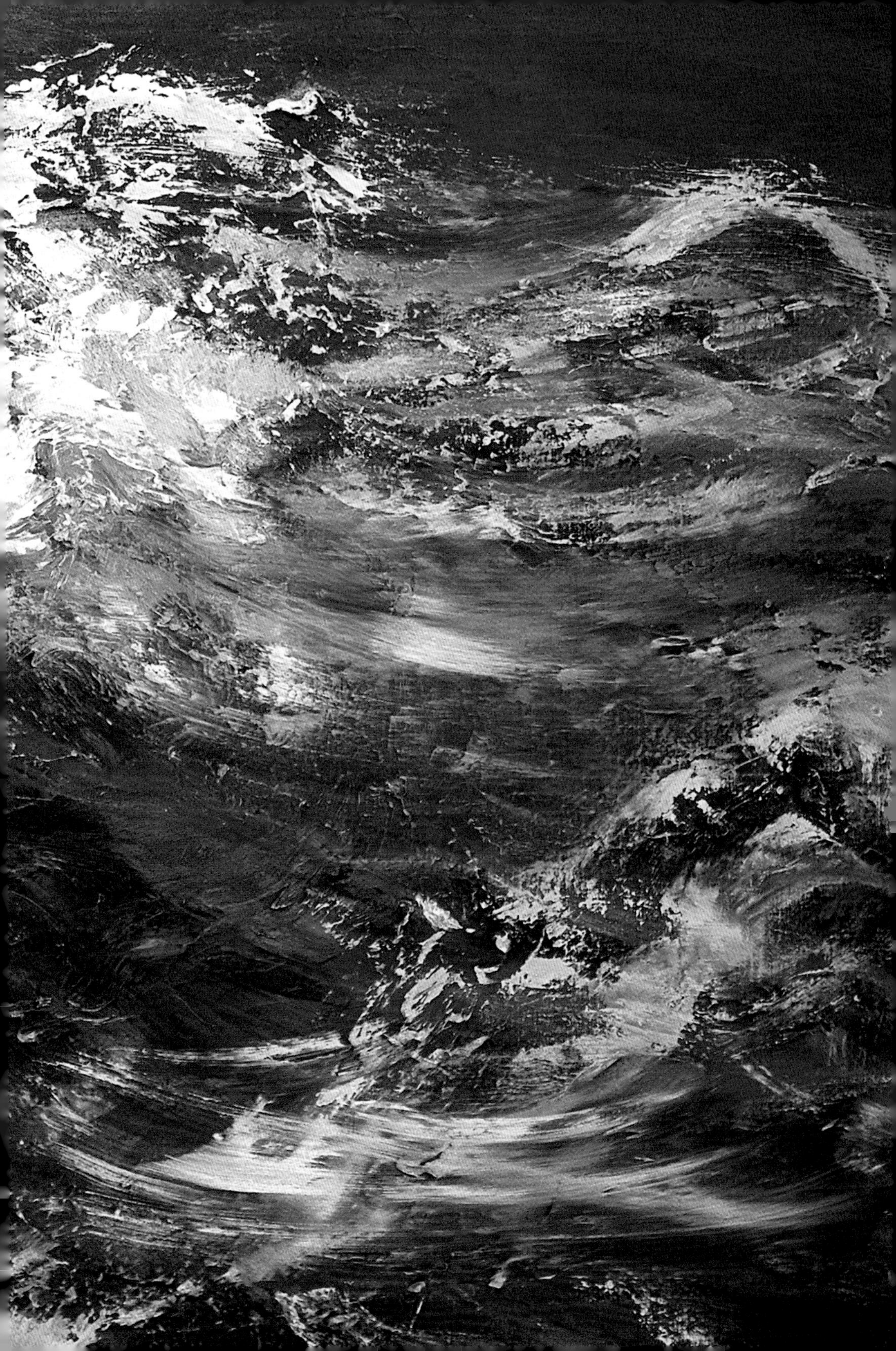

Memory of a storm

On the morning of Sunday November 30th 2002 I drove to the sea at Thorpeness. A great storm was raging, in the sky and at sea, the waves lashing and crashing. I came back to the studio, where I was working on a portrait from memory of a London beggar, on a little canvas, 12"by 10". All around me the storm was still raging. I remembered the intense and dramatic experience of the wild sea at Thorpeness that morning, and it was much more alive inside me than what I was trying to do on the canvas. So directly on top of the portrait of the beggar I painted the first of my *North Sea Paintings*, a memory of the morning's storm.

That storm was eye-opening. The sea was roaring and I was silent. The contrast between the grandeur of the elements and my own small vulnerable presence could not have been starker. I needed to absorb, to observe and listen. When I make a painting or a sculpture I try to be a channel through which the subject can travel. If it's the sea, the sea is in charge of me. It dictates the marks I make. Sometimes with Turner I feel that his bravura brushwork has more to do with Turner than the sea, as opposed to Constable, where the paint is his honest, earthy, direct response to his subject. Whatever the subject, I try to get myself out of the way so that the truth of that subject can come through me into the work. As Brancusi said, "It's not difficult to make a work of art. The difficulty lies in being in the right state to do it."

Throughout this period I would drive to the sea each morning and look and listen. Not draw but experience, then come back to the studio and paint from memory. The paintings

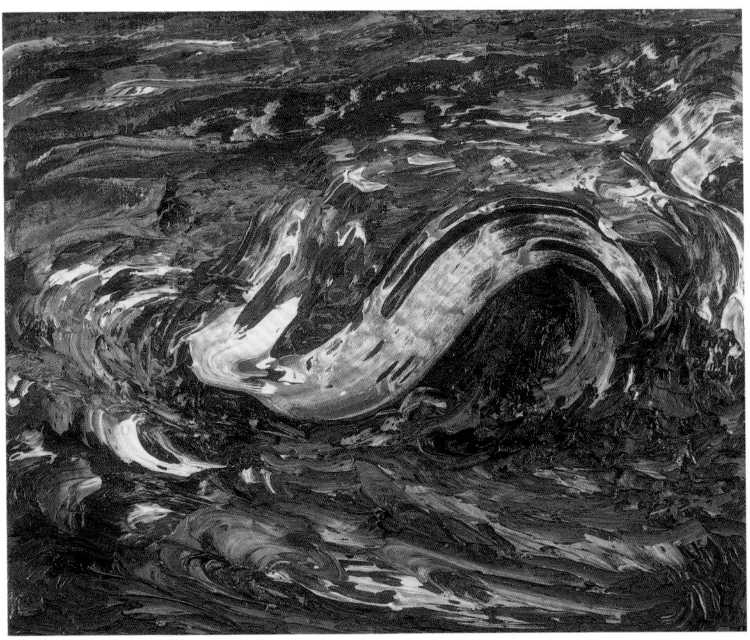

Rough sea, January, II, 2004, oil on canvas 25.4 x 30.5cm, private collection

accumulated. And then Jonathan Reekie came over to see them and suggested these first *North Sea Paintings* should be the Aldeburgh Festival Exhibition in 2003. The exhibition became an important factor in raising funds for *Scallop,* because those first little paintings—all small and vertical, as the first one had been—sold at £950, and £200 from each sale went into the *Scallop* fund.

Others, too, had begun to contribute. Friends like George Melly wrote to lots of people asking for support, and many responded. By this time the maquette for the sculpture was with Sam Pegg, made of real scallop shells. It was miniscule compared with the scale of the piece I wanted. No drawings, just the maquette; it would have been a lot easier for Peggs if there had been drawings. Each week I telephoned Sam to find out if there had been any progress, and each time Sam would say, "We've been looking at it." This went on for what seemed an unconscionable time.

By March 2003 we were about half-way there with the funding. Then something happened that persuaded me to take the plunge. I was in Aldeburgh looking up at the sky and suddenly I saw an unusual cloud formation. It was a very clear image of the wings of a flying bird moving through the sky. From that moment I had a huge sense of optimism that *Scallop* was going to happen.

You have to have faith. Occasionally you have to listen to a voice from somewhere else. And so, against the advice of everyone around me, I decided that we should begin.

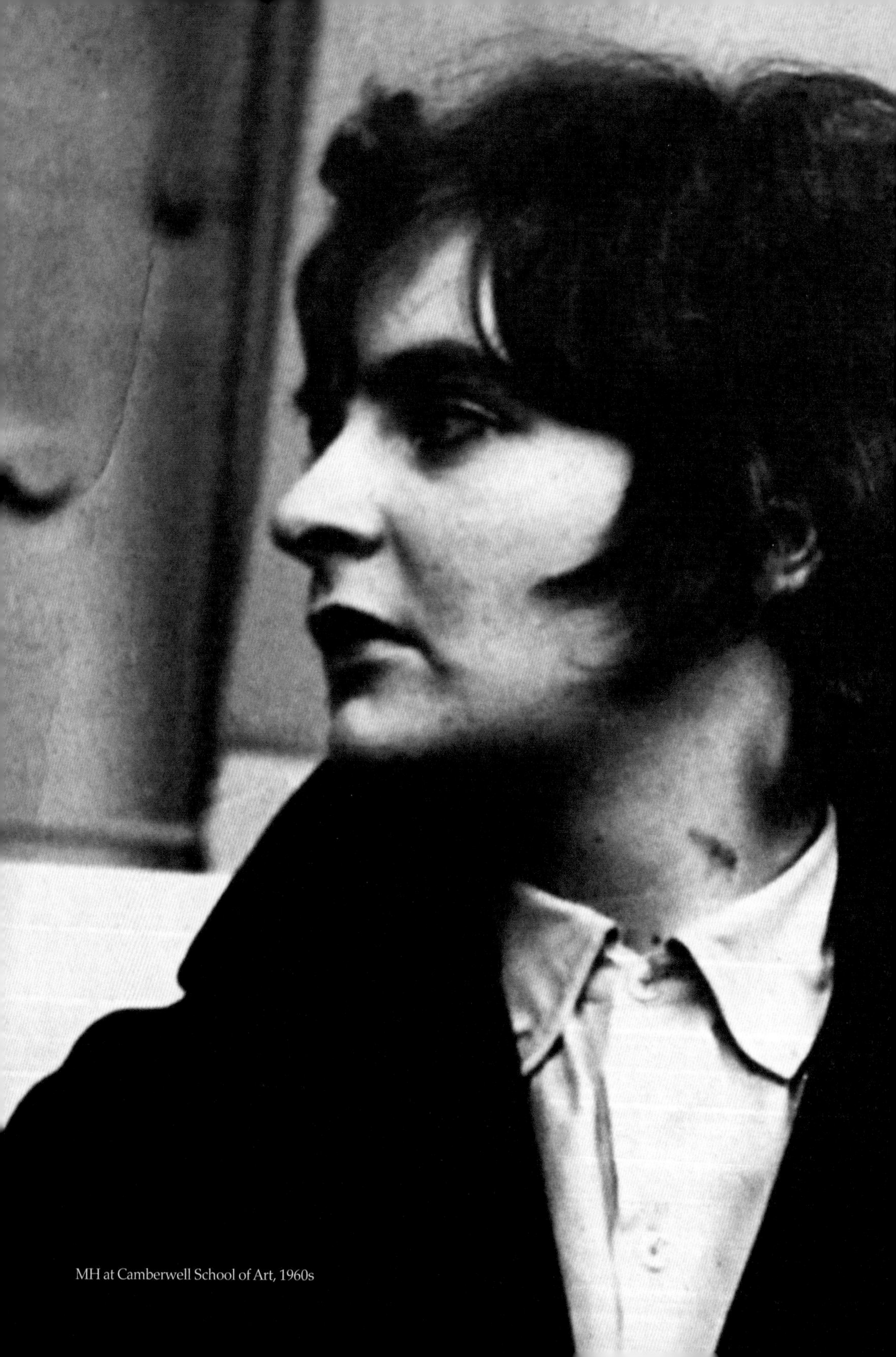

MH at Camberwell School of Art, 1960s

Part two: flashback

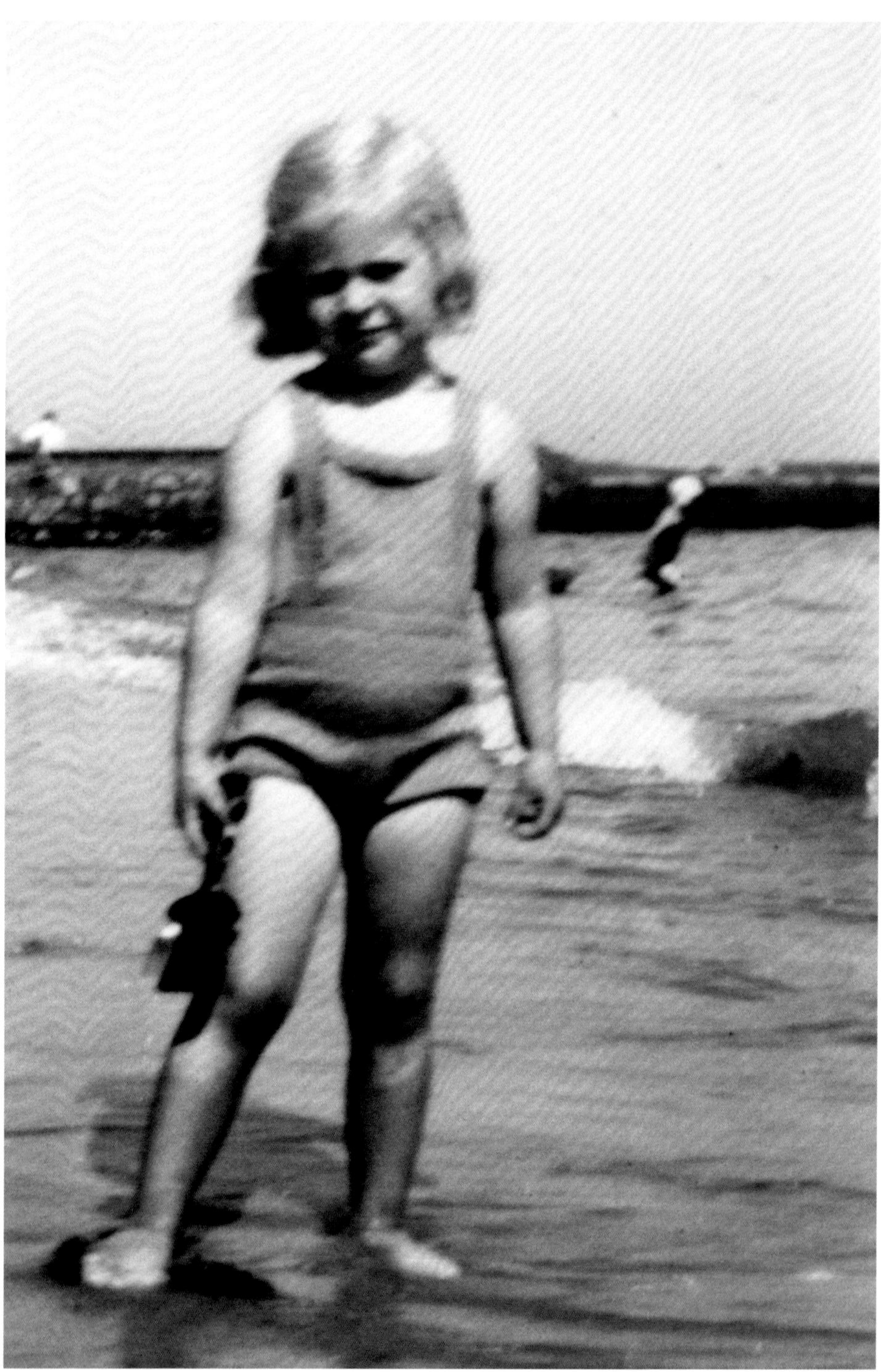

MH aged four

In the beginning was the sea

It all began with the sea. My mother took me there as a child. I wanted to go to Clacton, lots of funfairs, but she was rather snobbish and insisted on Frinton, which was more proper: no alcohol on the green sward.

I suppose I must have been quite an old toddler to be allowed to go into the sea by myself. I walked in and talked to it 10-to-the-dozen, as if it were my friend. I can't imagine what I said but I talked and talked. I also discovered the sounds of the sea in shells, but mostly I talked. Now I listen.

I'm a thoroughly Suffolk person. My father was born in Snape. Apparently there are 43 dead Hamblings in the churchyard there, and I now think that is where I shall go to join them, in time.

I was born in St Leonard's Hospital in Sudbury and grew up in Hadleigh. The town is in what I call the "domestic side" of Suffolk, as opposed to the "wild side", where I live now. It suits me better here. It's scruffier, and the sea majestic.

Becoming an artist happened by accident. I'd failed the entrance exam for Ipswich High School, where my sister Ann had been, and went instead to Amberfield in Nacton, near Ipswich—the "Dunces' School" I christened it, for girls who couldn't get into the High School. Amberfield was so-called because all around it were plantations of ghastly amber-coloured roses.

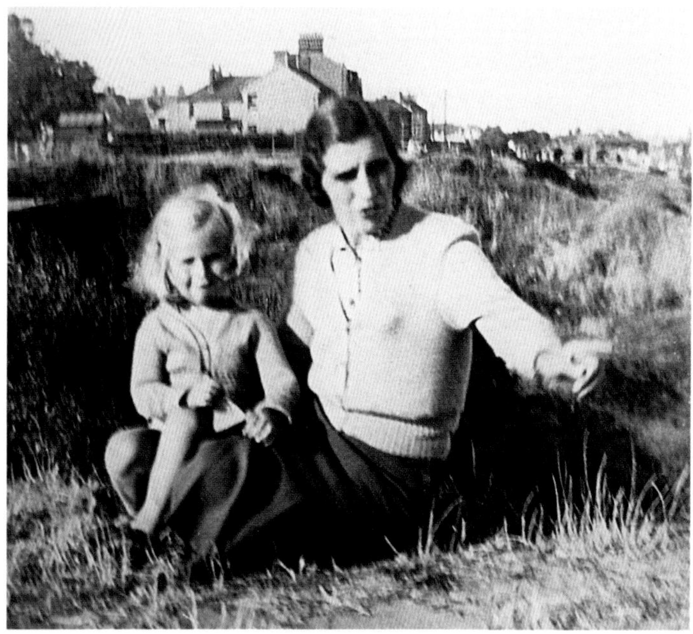

MH aged three with her mother in 1948

During the art exam when I was 14, I did nothing but flick paint about and generally draw attention to myself because I was deeply in love with the biology teacher, who was invigilating. Towards the end I suddenly noticed the clock, which said a quarter-past three, and I knew that at half-past I had to hand in a painting.

So I did one. There was a choice of three subjects, and, rather suitably I thought, I chose "Laziness". I painted a woman lounging on a chaise longue with an open book in her hand, but she was even too lazy to read it. And then two or three weeks later the results appeared and I came top.

It was an enormous surprise. Here was something that I was apparently good at without any effort or application. This was interesting. I remember staying up until 2 in the morning trying to paint the night sky out of my bedroom window in Hadleigh, and taking the paintings with me to school the next day. They were laid out on a table. I was on the point of tears because all the girls were laughing at them.

Then something happened without which my whole career might never have begun. Yvonne Drewry, a professional artist (whom we knew as Mrs Campbell), came into the room, noticed my distress and asked me what the matter was. I said I'd done these paintings the night before and that the girls were laughing at them.

She took me to one side and said, "Well, *I* think you're an artist, and whatever the reaction to your work might be, it should be as water off a duck's back. No matter

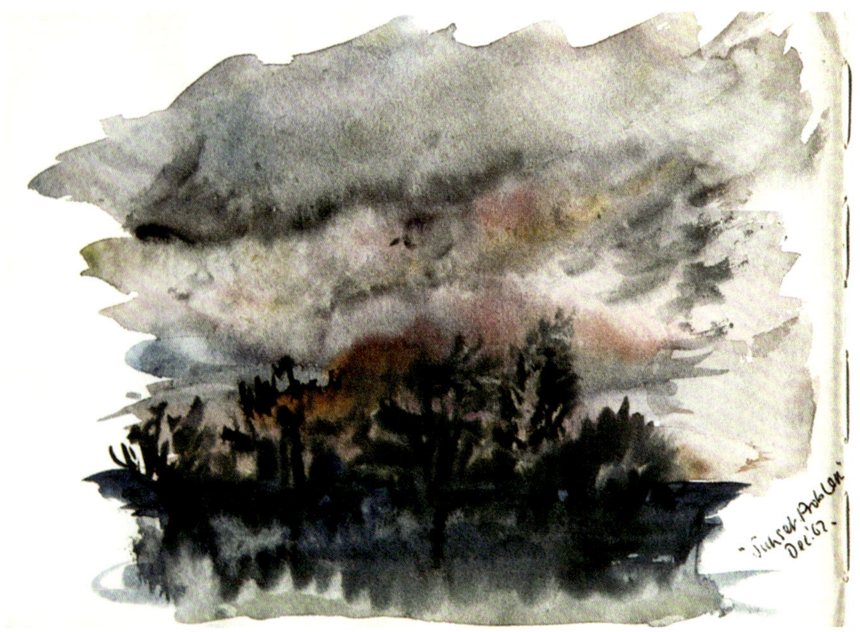

Sunset Problem, 1962, watercolour on paper 17.5 x 25cm, private collection

what it is, you should never let it affect you. You are your own best critic, so you have to grow a thicker skin."

I had previously had ideas of going on the stage, but Yvonne Drewry said that if I did, I'd be lucky to work a couple of weeks a year. "But I think you're an artist, and that means that no matter how poor you are you can always afford a pencil and paper." That made sense to me. Her own work, in watercolour, printmaking or oil paint, was alive and full of air and colour.

My mother bought me my first set of oil paints and I started. She paid for me to stay with Yvonne Drewry for a week during the Easter holiday to learn how to use them. That was also when I learned to smoke. Drewry lived in Kirton, on the way to Felixstowe. It was a hot day, I was in a field, and there were insects everywhere—on the palette, the brushes, the painting. She wandered across the field to see what I was doing and I shrugged in frustration and pointed to the insects sticking everywhere. "Ah," she said, "there's only one thing to do. Have a cigarette." That made sense to me too, so from the moment I had oil paints in my hands, I also had a cigarette.

Gin and French at Benton End

I had decided I would try to be an artist. But my parents felt they needed some validation of my promise other than that of Yvonne Drewry, so I took my first two oil paintings to Benton End, on the outskirts of Hadleigh, and notorious for every vice under the sun. It was known locally as the "Artists' House", because it was inhabited by such strange people. My parents knew of Sir Cedric Morris.

In fact, of course, Cedric Morris and Arthur Lett-Haines were famous, in Cedric's case not only as an artist but also as a gardener and plantsman. Cedric made grand, idiosyncratic and exotic oil paintings of birds, flowers, still life and, best of all for me, truly living portraits. Lett called himself an "English Surrealist". He constantly experimented with ideas and media and had a highly advanced imagination. For many of us, Cedric was the painter but Lett the artist. Together they had established the East Anglian School of Painting and Drawing, first in Dedham in Essex in 1937, then The Pound in Higham, in Suffolk, and finally Benton End in 1940. It was a large rambling farmhouse painted in pig's blood terra cotta with dark blue woodwork overlooking the valley of the River Brett.

I arrived at Benton End and knocked. It was a warm summer evening. Lett opened the door. He was very tall and rather frightening. I said, "Is Sir Cedric Morris at home?" "Cedric Morris is having his dinner," Lett replied. "May I wait?" I asked. "Well, you'd better come in," said Lett. He could see, I suppose, that having arrived, paintings under my arm, I wasn't going to go away.

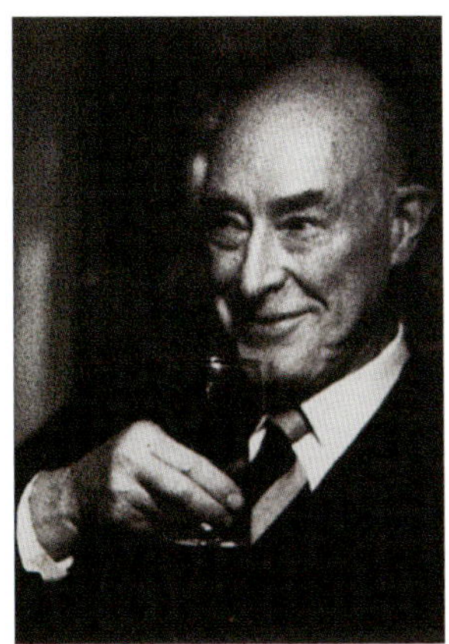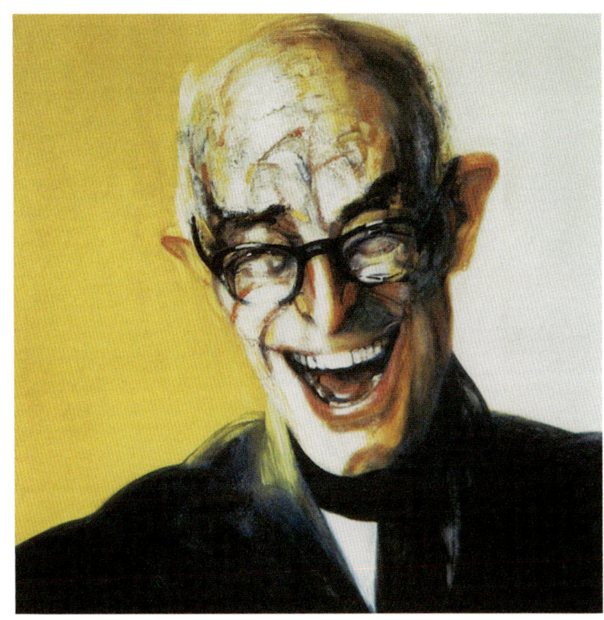

Above left: Authur Lett-Haines, 1969
Above right: *Lett laughing*, 1975-6, oil on board, 71 x 64.8cm, private collection

Cedric was indeed having dinner. Lett was not eating but had a big drink in his hand which I learned later to be a gin and French, always a gin and French, and he brought Cedric dish after dish. I'd never seen anything quite like it. Cedric sat the end of a long refectory table. He was very giggly, charming and sweet, and at the end of dinner he asked me to put my two paintings up on a storage heater where he could look at them. They were my first Suffolk landscapes, both studies of trees in the landscape at Kirton which I'd painted when I stayed with Yvonne Drewry. Cedric made criticisms but was encouraging. Then Lett came back into the room, another large gin and French in hand, and made opposite criticisms. That too was encouraging.

By this time it was nearly 10 o'clock in the evening and I was certain my mother must have decided that I had at the very least been sold off into the white slave trade, so I said I'd better go home. Lett supposed rightly that I was still at school, and said, "Well, come and paint in the holidays."

So I was there, with my paints, on the first day of the summer holidays. But I was too nervous to go up to the house, and painted in the ditch at the end of the drive until the painter Lucy Harwood came out of the back door ringing an enormous cow bell and calling my name. I went in, and that was really where, for me, in 1960 at the age of 15, life began.

How I found my best friend

At Benton End I worked in the kitchen with Lett and painted upstairs in the "Classroom". Lett taught me crucial things, the most important being that I must make my work my best friend. A friend I could go to whatever state I was in, whether I was miserable, whether I was happy, whether I was tired, bored or randy, whatever my state of mind I could always go to it, have a conversation with it as one would with a best friend who is always there for you. What a marvellous thing to be told at the age of 15! And that's how I've lived my life.

A bit later he said another important thing. "There's no point at all," he said, "in someone trying to be an artist if he or she has no imagination."

Lett was a man of extremes. I remember it became the fashion for noses to be altered. He objected strongly. "What's the point?" he said. "Everyone will just end up looking the same. If you have a big nose, keep it. If you're queer, be very queer."

I asked him once what it felt like to be in love—how you could tell you were in love. "Well," he said, "I can tell *you've* never been in love." I asked him how he knew that. "Because you wouldn't ask me the question." On another occasion I asked him what an aphrodisiac was. "Well," he said, "some people say shark fin soup, but personally, nothing beats a bit of rare bloody steak."

And he had a wonderful laugh, which seemed to move through an entire octave. This could have rather alarming consequences, since, being a little vain, he had

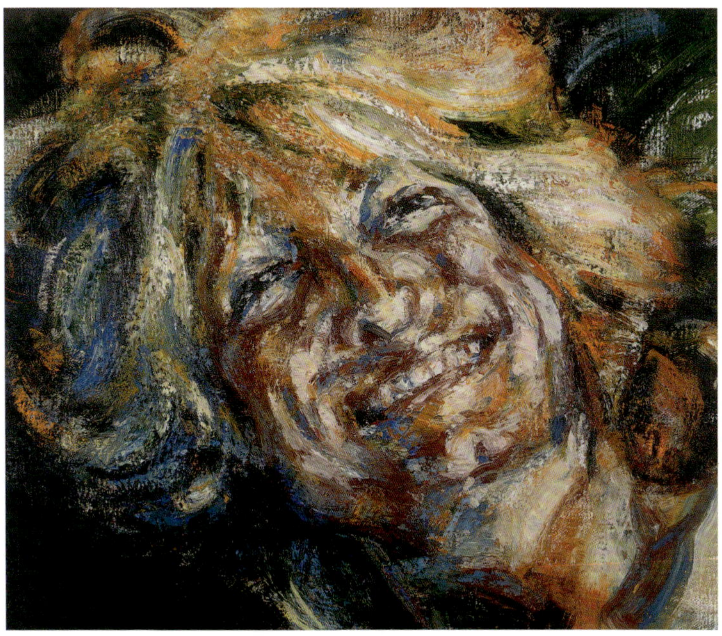

Tory laughing, 1984, oil on canvas 25.4 x 30.5cm, private collection

decided that National Health dentures would do him no favours, so had designed his own false teeth. The trouble was, they didn't fit, so when he laughed there was a perilous moment just before the teeth dropped. I use photographs only very rarely but one of the occasions on which I have done so was for *Lett laughing* (p.35): that photograph was taken at the moment just before the descent. The only other time I've used a photograph of someone laughing was of Tory. Laughter is such a strange, fleeting thing. It happens, and then in a second it's gone. Max Wall was the only person who could pose for me laughing convincingly for three quarters of an hour while I drew him.

A lot of people were frightened of Lett, which was why he was ironically called "Father". Incidentally, it was Lett who re-christened me "Maggi". He left a note on my chair in the Classroom saying, "This seat is still hot with the seat of Maggi Soop". Maggi, without an "e", as in the stock cube. He was a great teacher whom I loved very much. He was a *real* teacher in that when he took on a new pupil he would address himself completely to that person and bring out who that person was as an artist. It quickly became clear to me that you were either a Lett person or a Cedric person. Cedric people painted very much as Cedric did, whereas if you were a Lett person he would go to great lengths to help you find out who *you* were as an artist. I believe that is the mark of a true teacher. It is certainly how I have always tried to teach.

The fame bit

I left school half-way through A-Levels, depriving the headmistress of the pleasure of asking my parents to remove me, which I sensed was on the cards. As art had by now become my life, I went to Ipswich Art School for two years, but returned to Benton End at weekends and during holidays, still working with Lett and painting there. Then came three years at Camberwell, and two at the Slade: seven years altogether.

Among the teachers at Ipswich I remember in particular were Lawrence Self and Colin Moss. Self was an exciting, painterly painter of landscape, with a laconic sense of humour, Moss an expressionist of nudes, workers and towns. He'd been in the army and ran the Life Room with military discipline, which was a good thing. And Ipswich was enlightened in that you worked in a different discipline each day of the week: one day sculpture, one day pottery, one day life drawing, one day etching and one day something called Basic Design—very boring. This variety of possibilities was a good thing because one could make up one's own mind.

Robert Medley was Head of Painting at Camberwell. He was an artist of sensitivity and perception who had told his friend Wystan Auden at Greshams' School in Norfolk that he should write poetry. Robert was enlightened, we had huge freedom, and he aimed to give each of us by the end of three years the present of our own personality. We remained close friends until his death in 1994. Tory and I visited him in hospital the night before he died. Tory inadvertently kicked over his urine bottle, which amused him a lot. He was chatty

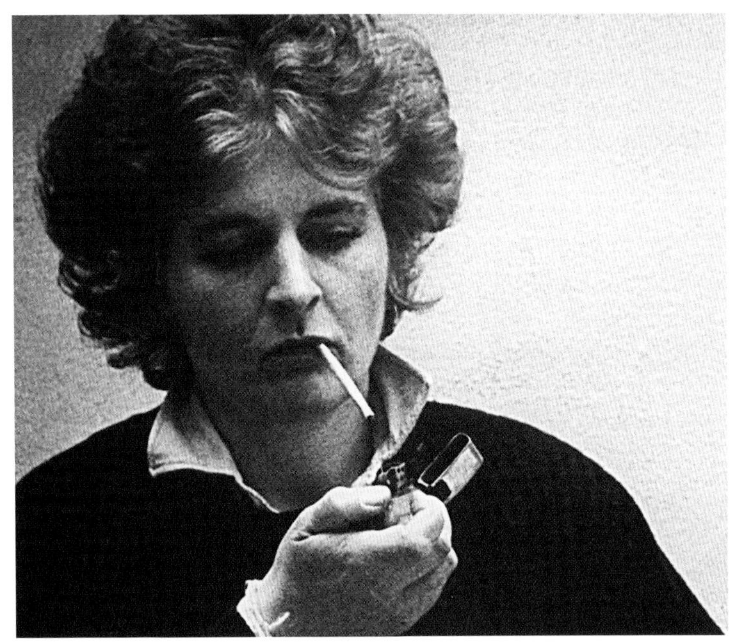

MH in the 1970s

and jolly until a young male nurse entered the ward. We were summarily dismissed and his last words to us in a loud whisper as the young man approached were, "Isn't he pretty? He comes from Norwich." At Camberwell I made various forays into Pop and Op Art and Abstract Expressionism, the fashion of the '60s, but worked consistently in the Life Room.

At the Slade I had abandoned painting by the end of the first term, and spent the rest of my time there building one of the first audio-visual environments, making street-works and performing in Marc Chaimowicz's anarchic dramas.

I left the Slade in 1969, having been lucky enough to be a student in the days of grants, not loans, before Mrs Thatcher contrived to close down Fine Art Departments in favour of Graphic Design, more commercial. I realized how much I missed the feel of oil paint, was bored by conceptual art, and returned in 1970 to painting. My first show in London was in 1973 at Morley Gallery, part of Morley College, where I had begun to teach. I had half the gallery and my friend Jane Joseph, who had also been at Camberwell and also taught at Morley, had the other half. My paintings were portraits of lone figures done from memory of people in pubs, and pretty amazingly they sold out. I would go to a pub and if I found someone who moved me, I would try to commit him or her to memory rather than draw. I trained my visual memory then, in those pubs, observing those people very, very keenly, then going straight home to the studio to paint. After that show at Morley I was chosen to be in "British Painting '74" at the Hayward Gallery. That's where the fame bit really began.

Called to the "wild side"

My move to the "wild side" of Suffolk was thanks largely to Anglia Television and mascara. In 1987 I had an exhibition at the Serpentine. Anglia in those days produced a series called *Folio*—their version of the South Bank Show—and they made an hour-long programme about me. This was seen by someone called Lady Gwatkin, who wrote me a fan letter asking that if I ever showed work in East Anglia would I invite her.

So I did. There was an exhibition at the Peter Pears Gallery in Aldeburgh chosen by Peter Fuller and she saw that. Then in 1988 my watercolours and drawings from the Serpentine went on to the Minories in Colchester. The Minories was large and prestigious in those days, and my work filled only half of it. They asked me what to hang in the other half and I said, "Why not show my father?" Father, who had been Chief Cashier in the Hadleigh branch of Barclays, took up painting at 65 after retiring at 60. He was a terrific painter—the whole of Suffolk was inside him and it just poured out. So we had the Harry and Maggi Show. Father sold everything and I sold one watercolour—bought by Lady Gwatkin.

Later that summer Father and I delivered the painting to her. It was a Suffolk sunrise. She then proceeded to send me photographs of her watermeadows (she had bought land around her cottage so that it wouldn't be built on) and in season, local asparagus wrapped in wet newspaper in Jiffy bags, and the occasional crate of Adnams champagne. She was very keen that when in Suffolk I should come to dinner.

I always spent the second week of August with my parents in Hadleigh. I'd get up early

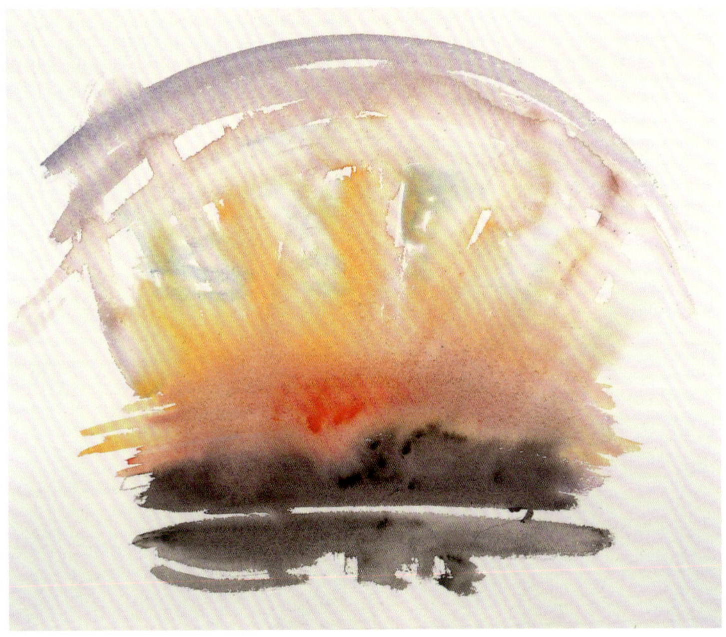

July sunrise, Orwell Estuary 7, 1985, watercolour 48.3 x 61cm, private collection

and paint the sunrise. Eventually I did go to dinner with June Gwatkin, taking my dog Percy with me. The Gwatkin was very short, shorter even than I am. The top of her head was barely level with my tits. There was a lot of champagne and a lot of smoked salmon, and as I tried to leave, in order to get back to Hadleigh, she attempted what can only be described as something more than a social kiss. Percy, who was a Jack Russell, became "The Hound of the Baskervilles" and rose vertically from the floor, shooting into the air with lips back, snarling with fury.

I was already backing out of the front door and thought, "Oh well, no more fresh asparagus for me." But her offerings didn't stop. There were books on lady gardeners, a first edition by Oscar Wilde's mother, and then she began to write saying that she would like to leave her cottage and watermeadows to me.

This created a dilemma , and I didn't quite know what to do about it. But The Gwatkin believed that Suffolk land should go back to Suffolk people, and eventually my friend Deborah MacMillan, widow of Kenneth MacMillan, said, "Look, it's fate, you're meant to have this place. You've got to say yes." And so in the end I accepted. The last time I saw Lady Gwatkin was in the early summer of 1994 at Christchurch Mansion in Ipswich, where my exhibition *Towards Laughter* was about to open. We had tea at the White Horse Hotel and then she tootled off. She died the following October, leaving me her cottage and watermeadows, within 15 minutes of the sea.

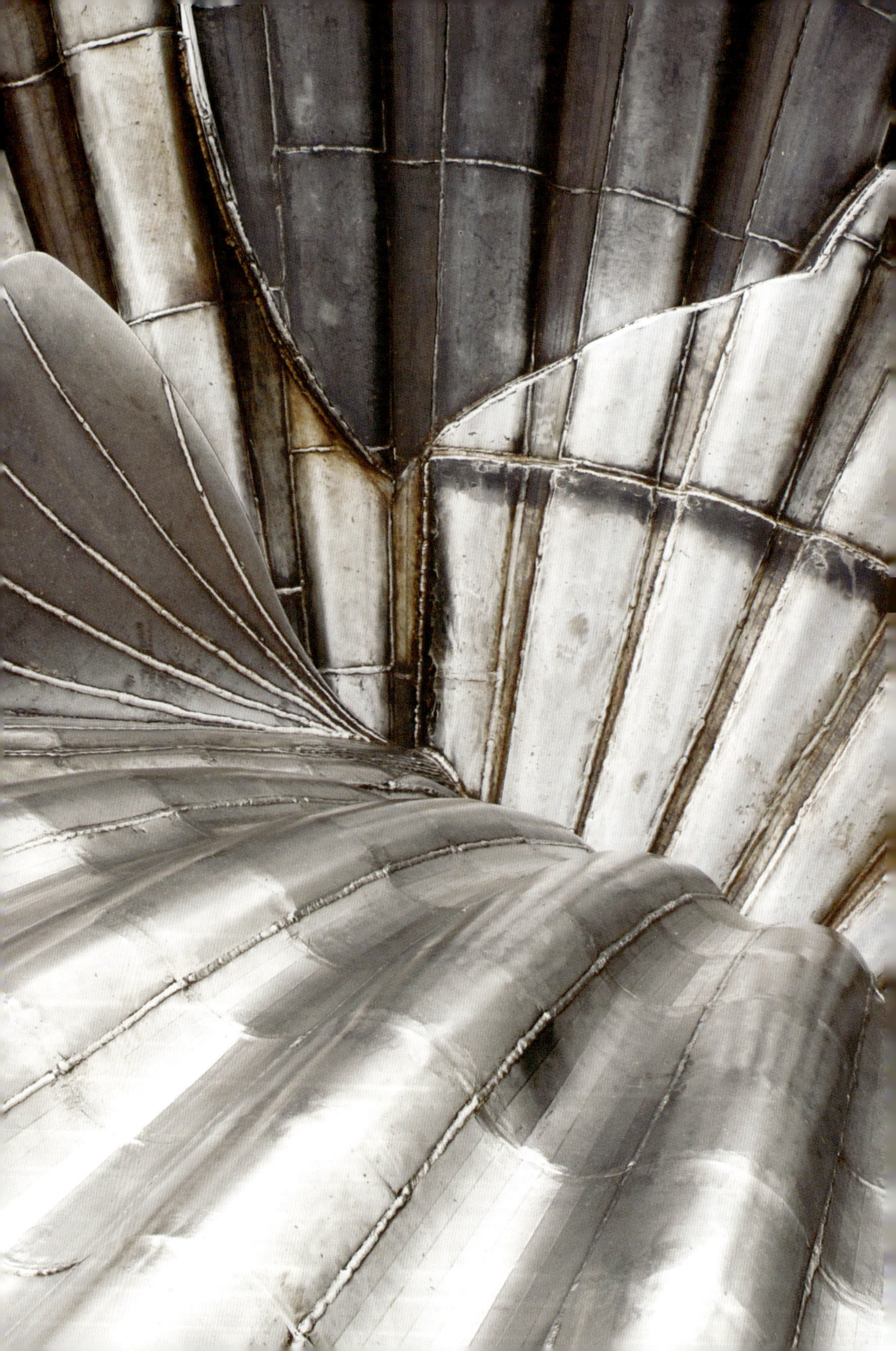

Part three: fast forward

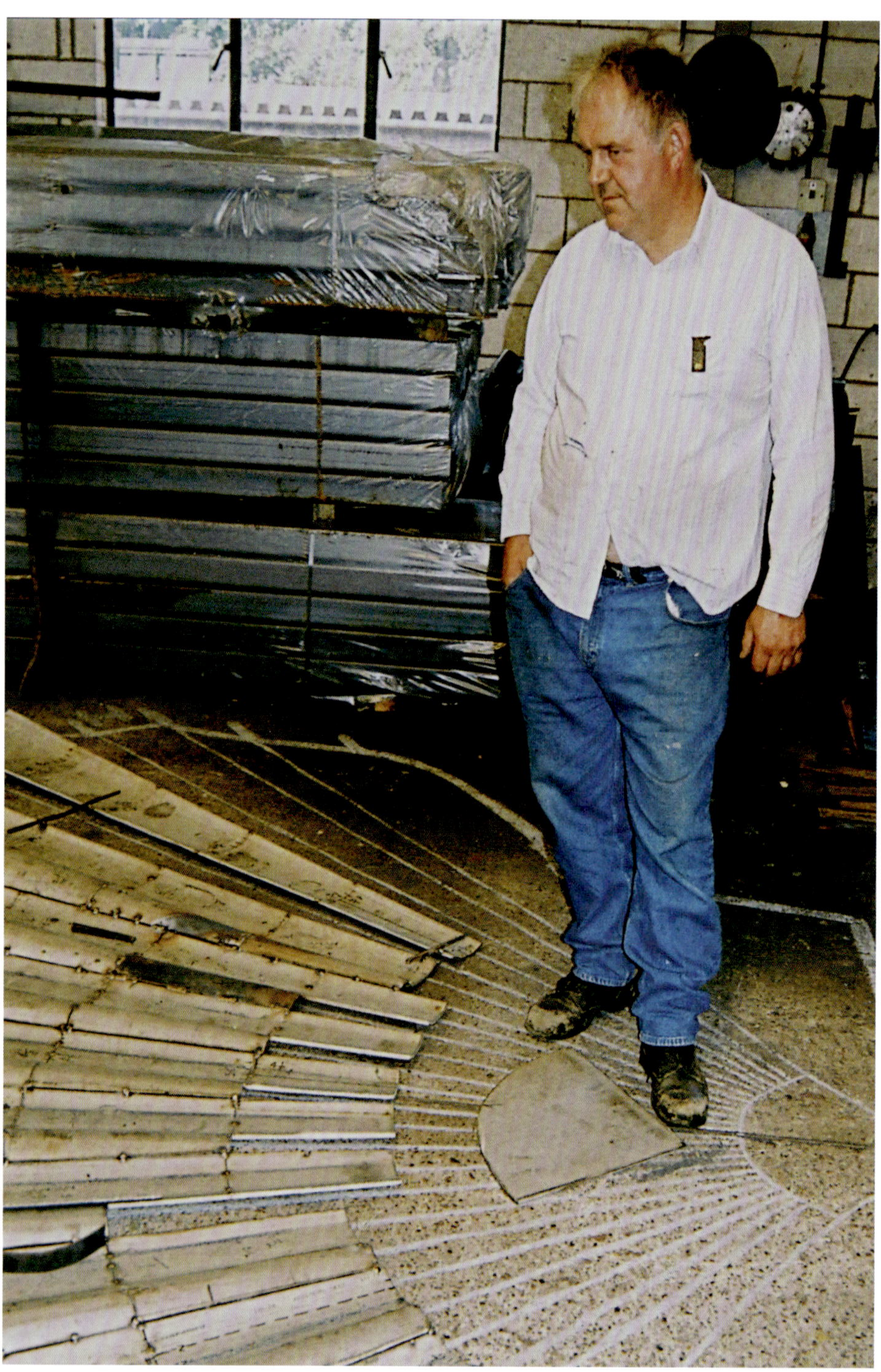
Sam Pegg ponders

A shell shattered and remade

It is early 2003. The maquette is in the Peggs' workshop, and Sam is repeating his mantra "We've been looking at it…"

But then somehow the *East Anglian Daily Times* got wind that something might be brewing in Aldeburgh. One of their reporters, Sarah Chambers, telephoned me to say that she'd heard that a Benjamin Britten sculpture was in the making and asked whether she could come over to photograph it and talk to Sam and me. I rang Sam and said, "Look, the *East Anglian* is coming on Friday. Can you produce something?" Sam set to at last, and for the *East Anglian's* first visit we had four long curves of a section of the shell. We set them rising up from the floor and going over a trestle to suggest some feeling of movement.

On the appointed day I arrived early and, knowing that Sam and his son Dennis were inclined to be more taciturn than loquacious, I said to them, "We must all be very enthusiastic and excited about this." Sarah Chambers arrived and we showed her into the workshop to have a look at the small hastily assembled sections of the shell. I explained what it was that I had in mind, and she took out her notebook and turned to Sam and asked, "What do you think it's going to be like when it's a work of art on the beach?" Sam paused for what felt like 20 minutes. "I reserve judgment on that," he said at last. Sadly she didn't put that into her article.

But the *East Anglian* had played its part in getting things going. At last we were on

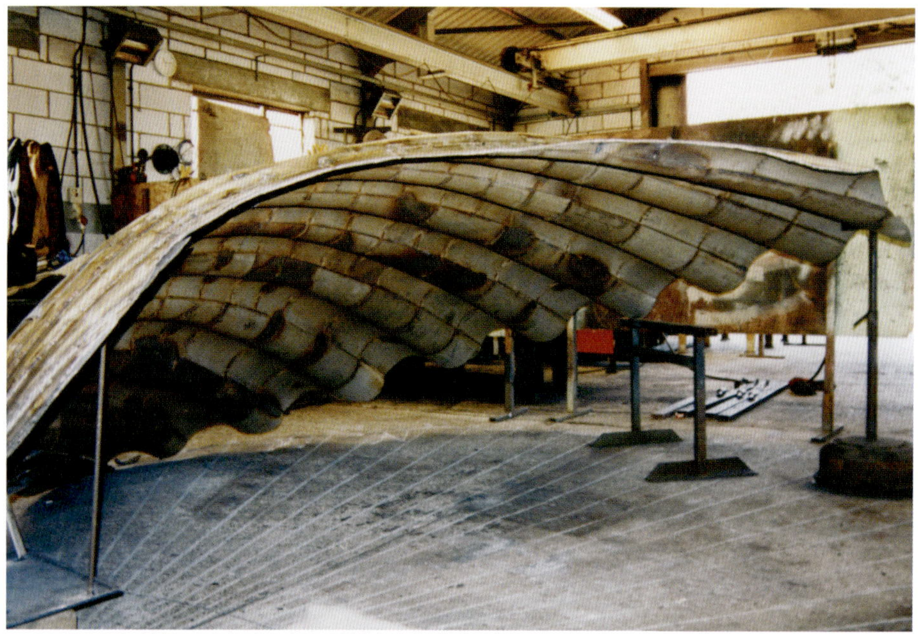

Early fabrication in the Peggs' workshop, Aldeburgh

our way. It then became apparent just how big a challenge *Scallop* was going to be in engineering terms. And I realized just what impressive engineers and craftsmen Sam and Dennis are. They had never done anything like this before. Nor had I. My only previous public sculpture, *A Conversation with Oscar Wilde* (facing Charing Cross Station in London), is granite and bronze. For *Scallop* Sam insisted on 10mm stainless steel, to enable it to withstand the marine environment. But 10mm stainless steel is extremely difficult to work with. Each small section, about 30cm by 15cm, had to be individually measured and made, then taken to a machine that could bend it in just the right way. These sections were then welded together to create the complex forms of the sculpture.

It took Sam and Dennis seven months, Dennis working full-time. I worked on it too, and Sam was always there wrestling with the problems. One such problem was presented by the fact that the vertical part of the sculpture was split. Sam worried that if a rugger team decided to get up on to the horizontal part, took hold of the vertical section and "gave it some welly", it might not stand the pressure. So he devised the buttresses, the diagonal bands that hold the split vertical together. I was very much against them at first, but Sam insisted. Now I like them very much and think they add to the energy of the image of the shell shattering. This moment of action is what I try to achieve in my paintings of waves breaking: something as sudden as falling in love. Together with Andrew Hawes, Sam determined how the sculpture would be installed

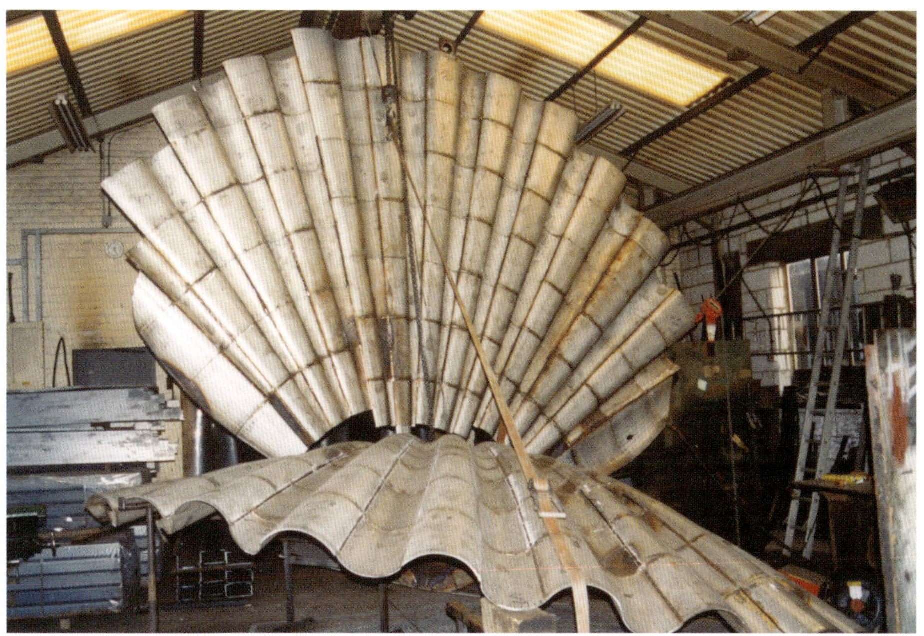

in the shingle in such a way that no one could pick it up and walk off with it.

Just as there were different elements of form in *Scallop*, I wanted differences of colour: part of it shining, part of it dark and rusty and part a combination of the two. The shining element presented no problem: stainless steel polishes brilliantly. But how to achieve a dark, rust-like patina? We had a piece of stainless steel in Peggs' yard and for weeks experimented with all kinds of chemicals, but to no avail. Finally it was Sam who had the idea of cutting the vertical part of the shell into three sections and taking them to Lowestoft for heat-treatment. The baking process created the dark brown rusty look I wanted.

What I was trying to achieve was a contrast between the polished steel shining where it faces the sea and catches the sun and the strange dark silhouette rusting as it thrusts up through the shingle. The under-side of the curved shell I wanted as dark as possible, as if it were under the sea, the underbelly of a wave. I wanted light and dark, life and death, and movement between colours as between forms.

But each time I went to Peggs during the manufacture of *Scallop* I was full of terror. You never know whether, or how, things are going to work out until you're finished. Usually my sense of foreboding proved to be quite unnecessary. Apart from the arguments about buttresses, each time I arrived the sculpture had gone one step further and was taking shape beautifully.

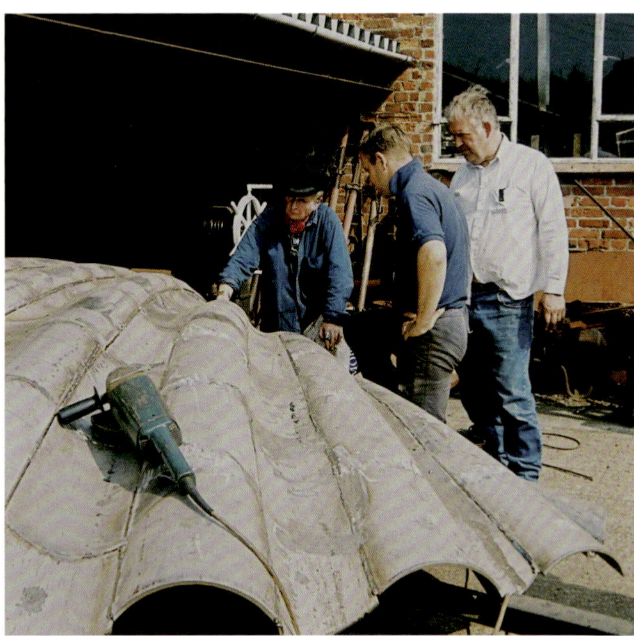

MH, Dennis and Sam in discussion in the yard

I came to understand the importance of good engineering. It was my first encounter with any form of engineering. Sam was extremely knowledgeable on the subject, and I began to understand his insistence on making *Scallop* strong.

Sculpture is often a collaborative effort and a very long, slow process. It's one thing to be alone in my studio painting, quite another making a sculpture with other people. It's a wonderful change when you're working with sympathetic people. Whatever the difficulties and challenges, we all became more and more excited as *Scallop* began to take shape.

Late in the summer *Scallop* was moved out of the workshop into Peggs' yard. She was almost complete. There, where one could see the sky though the words, it became really exciting and much less terrifying. But I remained nervous. Until *Scallop* was installed on the beach I was full of nerves and doubts. Self-doubt is a huge part of being an artist.

<h1 style="text-align:right">Slow grind</h1>

Meanwhile there was that other small matter, obtaining planning permission for *Scallop* to be installed on the beach. There were many long meetings with Suffolk Coastal. The friendly, quietly optimistic voice of John Davies (their Countryside and Information Manager) on the telephone was a continuous comfort. We had also to apply to English Nature, because that stretch of beach is part of the Heritage Coast. And the Sea Pea grows there. Apparently some centuries ago the Sea Pea helped Aldeburgh to keep going during a period of famine, and if *Scallop* were to intrude upon its domain there would be trouble.

A meeting took place on the beach with Simon Loftus, Maggy Wilson, Judith Forde (President of the Aldeburgh Society at the time) and a man from English Nature. Simon and Judith are both very tall, Maggy Wilson and I very short. The man looked to me, as most people do nowadays, about 12 years old, a short, nervous young man resembling a schoolboy. Happily there was no evidence of the Sea Pea on the small area of beach where *Scallop* was to go, and so English Nature could find no reason to object.

The final meeting took place at Suffolk Coastal. I believe only 20 or so members of the public turned up, and only one woman spoke against the sculpture. Suffolk Coastal voted unanimously in favour of *Scallop*.

And we were making progress in raising funds. The Norman Scarfe Trust

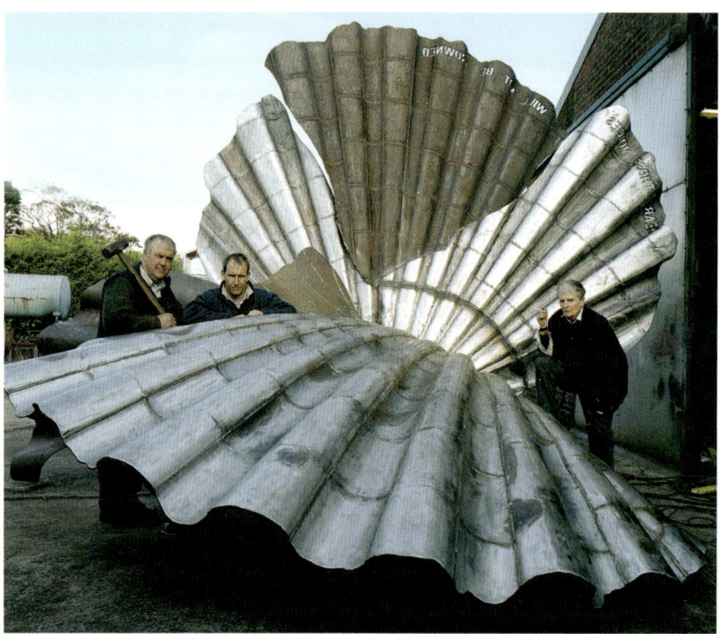

Sam, Dennis and MH with the finished sculpture

contributed generously, as did Eastern Arts and the Monument Trust, which had provided much of the funding for the Oscar Wilde sculpture in London. Individuals were contributing anything from £20 to £2,000, and that summer the sale of my *North Sea Paintings* at Snape Maltings added £24,000. Then, at the last minute, when we were still £13,000 short, the Foundation for Sport & the Arts weighed in thanks to the excellent Culture Secretary, Chris Smith, and the funding was in the bag.

A good use for agricultural fleece

And then at last, there in Peggs' yard, stood *Scallop,* complete. All three-and-a-half tons of her. She was hoisted by a crane on to one of Peggs' lorries, and at 7.30 on the morning of Thursday 6th November 2003 gradual progress was made down Park Road. Sam marched ahead like a man at the front of a funeral procession, holding aloft an enormously long pole with which to raise the telephone and electricity wires. Those wires were all quite relaxed, until the last one, which was taut. But Big Sam achieved the few millimetres necessary for *Scallop* on her lorry to squeeze underneath, just.

Then, very slowly, we proceeded down the High Street. It was November but marvellously clear weather and very few people about. And eventually we reached the beach. The foundations had been put in place the day before, a great steel tray two or three metres below ground with columns reaching up to receive *Scallop*. She was lowered by the crane on to the fixing points, and secured by enormous bolts. Then the JCB replaced four tons of shingle between the steel tray and *Scallop*. Sam had made sure that anyone who thought of stealing her would have a great deal of trouble.

The unveiling was due on Saturday the 8th, so the next problem was how to veil her. It was agreed that the only thing that would work was agricultural fleece. Great big rolls of white agricultural fleece. That Friday afternoon was particularly windy, but Dennis climbed to the top of *Scallop*. He was an amorphous moving shape under the fleece. It reminded me of that wonderful Henry Moore drawing, *Crowd looking*

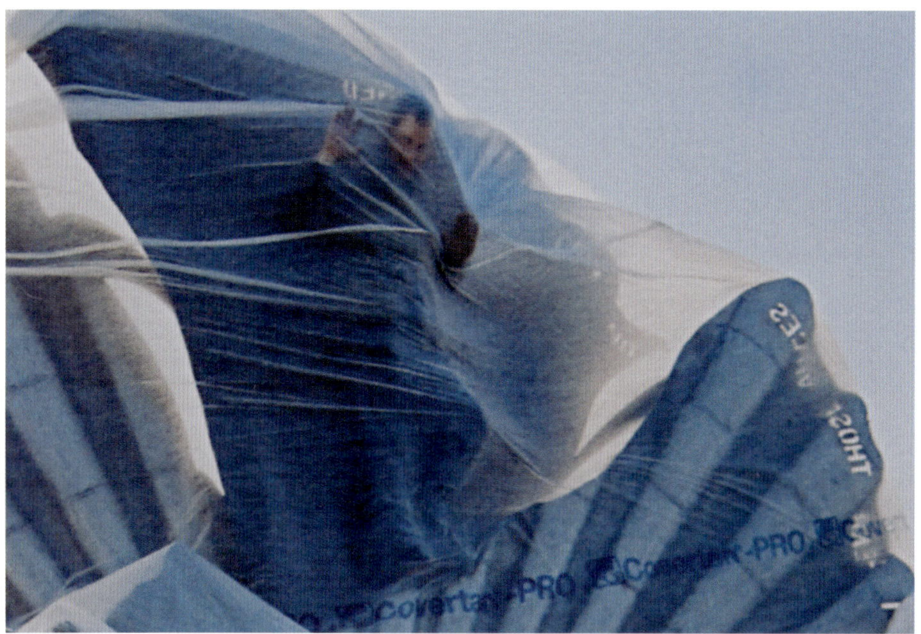

Dennis Pegg under the agricultural fleece

at a tied-up object. Finally everyone on the beach, including surprised passers-by, was asked to kneel around the shell to hold down the fleece. It was like an extraordinary kite flapping in the wind, but was finally tethered.

Around five o'clock, Dennis and I sat by *Scallop* waiting to be collected. We were pretty exhausted. Now came the first hint that there might be trouble ahead. From the car park an Aldeburgh lady, smart, stately and stern, marched across the shingle towards us. She halted.

"Is this the sculpture?" she asked.

I decided to say nothing and leave it to Dennis.

"This is it," said Dennis.

"Yes, I can see that," she continued. "It's been delivered, obviously. But where is it going?"

"This is it," said Dennis.

"Yes," she said, "I can see this is it. But where is it going?"

"This is it," said Dennis.

She finally got the message, and it was clearly undesirable. "Oh my God," she said, theatrically, hand to forehead. "Oh my God. I hoped it was going somewhere far less conspicuous than this. How dreadful." And she retreated muttering, back across the shingle to her car. It was an unforgettable moment.

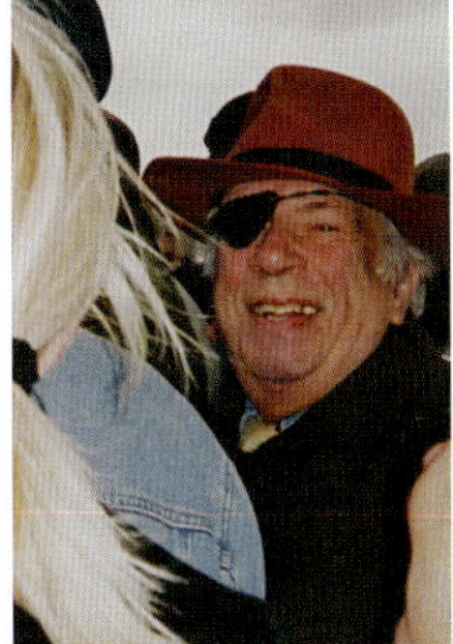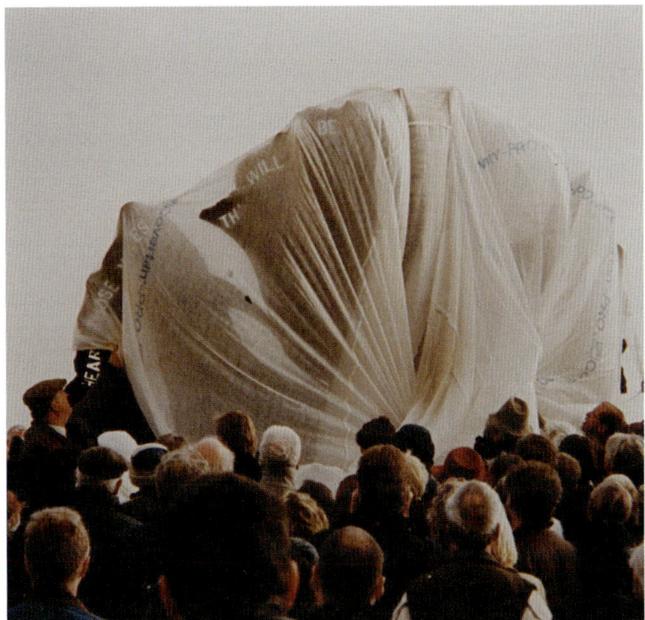

The crowd, including George Melly in his red fedora, awaits the unveiling, Saturday 8th November 2003

Scallop was unveiled at 12 noon on Saturday 8th November 2003. Invitations had been sent and a large crowd gathered. Chris Smith made a speech and pulled the magic cord. I gathered later—I didn't hear them then—that there were one or two dissenting shouts during Chris Smith's speech. I didn't notice. I just wanted the unveiling to be an unveiling because I'd had visions of the fleece refusing to leave the sculpture.

But off came the fleece and *Scallop* was unveiled, and Chris Smith formally handed her over to Suffolk Coastal District Council. The sun came out. There was a huge cheer, and we all repaired to Aldeburgh Primary School, opposite Peggs, where Adnams provided champagne. Later that night I gave a party in our village hall for everyone who had been involved. George Melly made a speech. I urged Sam to make one but he declined and so Dennis stood up. I thanked everyone. And *Scallop* was toasted again.

Then, very soon, all hell broke loose.

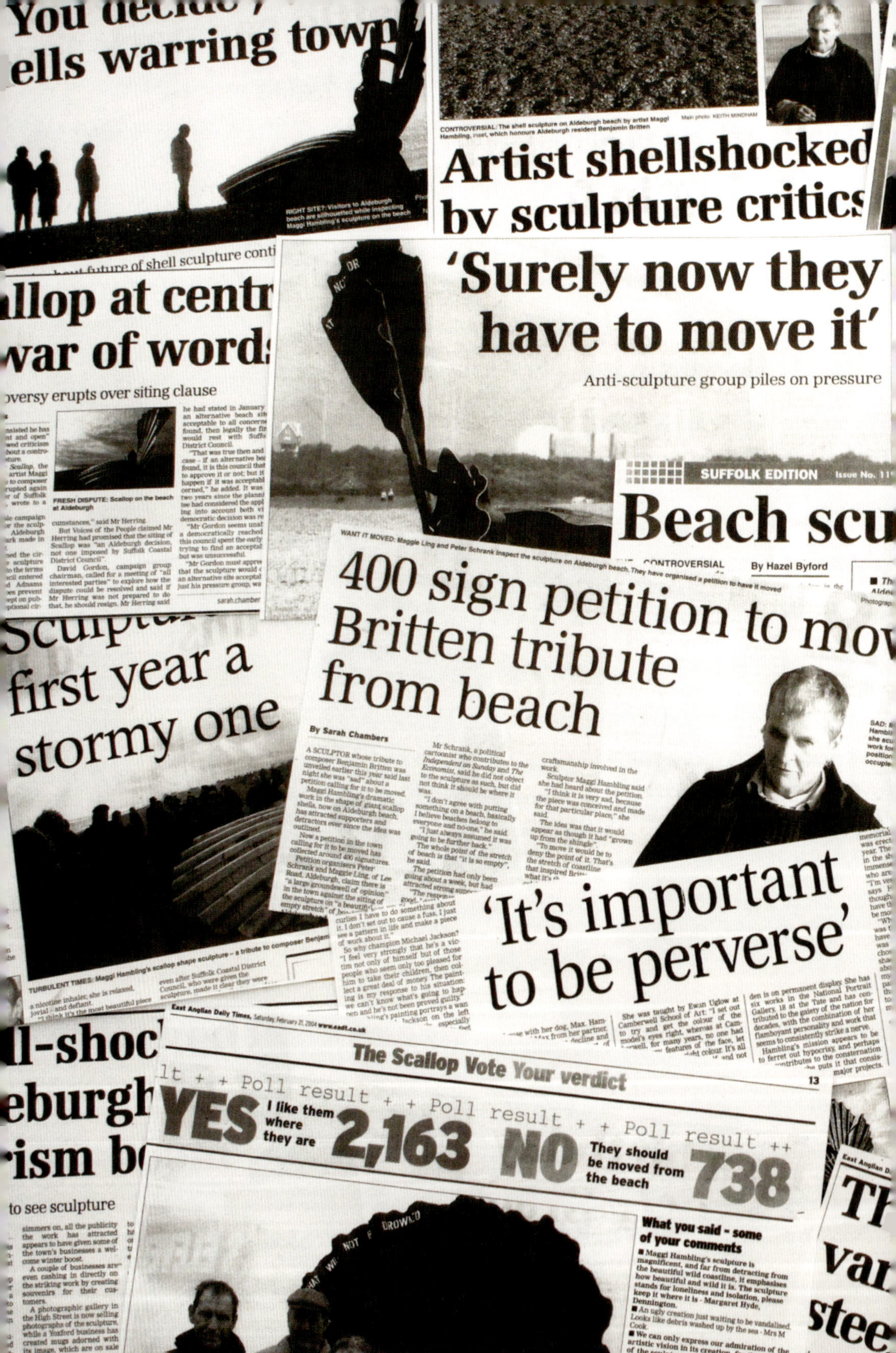
You decide
ells warring town
Artist shellshocked
by sculpture critics
CONTROVERSIAL: The shell sculpture on Aldeburgh beach by artist Maggi Hambling, inset, which honours Aldeburgh resident Benjamin Britten
Main photo: KEITH MINDHAM
'Surely now they
have to move it'
Anti-sculpture group piles on pressure
allop at centr
war of words
oversy erupts over siting clause
RIGHT SITE?: Visitors to Aldeburgh beach are silhouetted while inspecting Maggi Hambling's sculpture on the beach
FRESH DISPUTE: Scallop on the beach at Aldeburgh
SUFFOLK EDITION
Issue No. 11
Beach scu
CONTROVERSIAL
By Hazel Byford
WANT IT MOVED: Maggie Ling and Peter Schrank inspect the sculpture on Aldeburgh beach. They have organised a petition to have it moved
400 sign petition to mov
Britten tribute
from beach
By Sarah Chambers
'It's important
to be perverse'
Sculptur
first year a
stormy one
TURBULENT TIMES: Maggi Hambling's scallop shape sculpture – a tribute to composer Benjamin
East Anglian Daily Times, Saturday, February 21, 2004 www.eadt.co.uk
13
The Scallop Vote Your verdict
++ Poll result ++ + Poll result ++ + Poll result ++
YES
I like them where they are
2,163
NO
They should be moved from the beach
738
What you said – some of your comments
l-shock
eburgh
ism b
to see sculpture

400 sign petition to move Britten tribute from beach

By Sarah Chambers

A SCULPTOR whose tribute to composer Benjamin Britten was unveiled earlier this year said last night she was "sad" about a petition calling for it to be moved.

Maggi Hambling's dramatic work in the shape of giant scallop shells, now on Aldeburgh beach, has attracted supporters and detractors ever since the idea was outlined.

Now a petition in the town calling for it to be moved has collected around 400 signatures.

Petition organisers Peter Schrank and Maggie Ling, of Lee Road, Aldeburgh, claim there is "a large groundswell of opinion" in the town against the siting of the sculpture on "a beautiful empty stretch of bea

Mr Schrank, a political cartoonist who contributes to the Independent on Sunday and The Economist, said he did not object to the sculpture as such, but did not think it should be where it was.

"I don't agree with putting something on a beach, basically I believe beaches belong to everyone and no-one," he said.

"I just always assumed it was going to be further back."

"The whole point of the stretch of beach is that "it is so empty"," he said.

The petition had only been going about a week, but had attracted strong su

craftsmanship involved in the work.

Sculptor Maggi Hambling said she had heard about the petition.

"I think it is very sad, because the piece was conceived and made for that particular place," she said.

The idea was that it would appear as though it had "grown up from the shingle".

"To move it would be to deny the point of it." That's the stretch of coastline that inspired Brit

what it's

YES I like them where they are 2,163

NO They should be moved from the beach 738

What you said – some of your comments

■ Maggi Hambling's sculpture is magnificent, and far from detracting from the beautiful wild coastline, it emphasises how beautiful and wild it is. The sculpture stands for loneliness and isolation, please keep it where it is - Margaret Hyde, Dennington.

■ An ugly creation just waiting to be vandalised. Looks like debris washed up by the sea - Mrs M Cook

■ We can only express our admiration for the artistic vision in its creation for

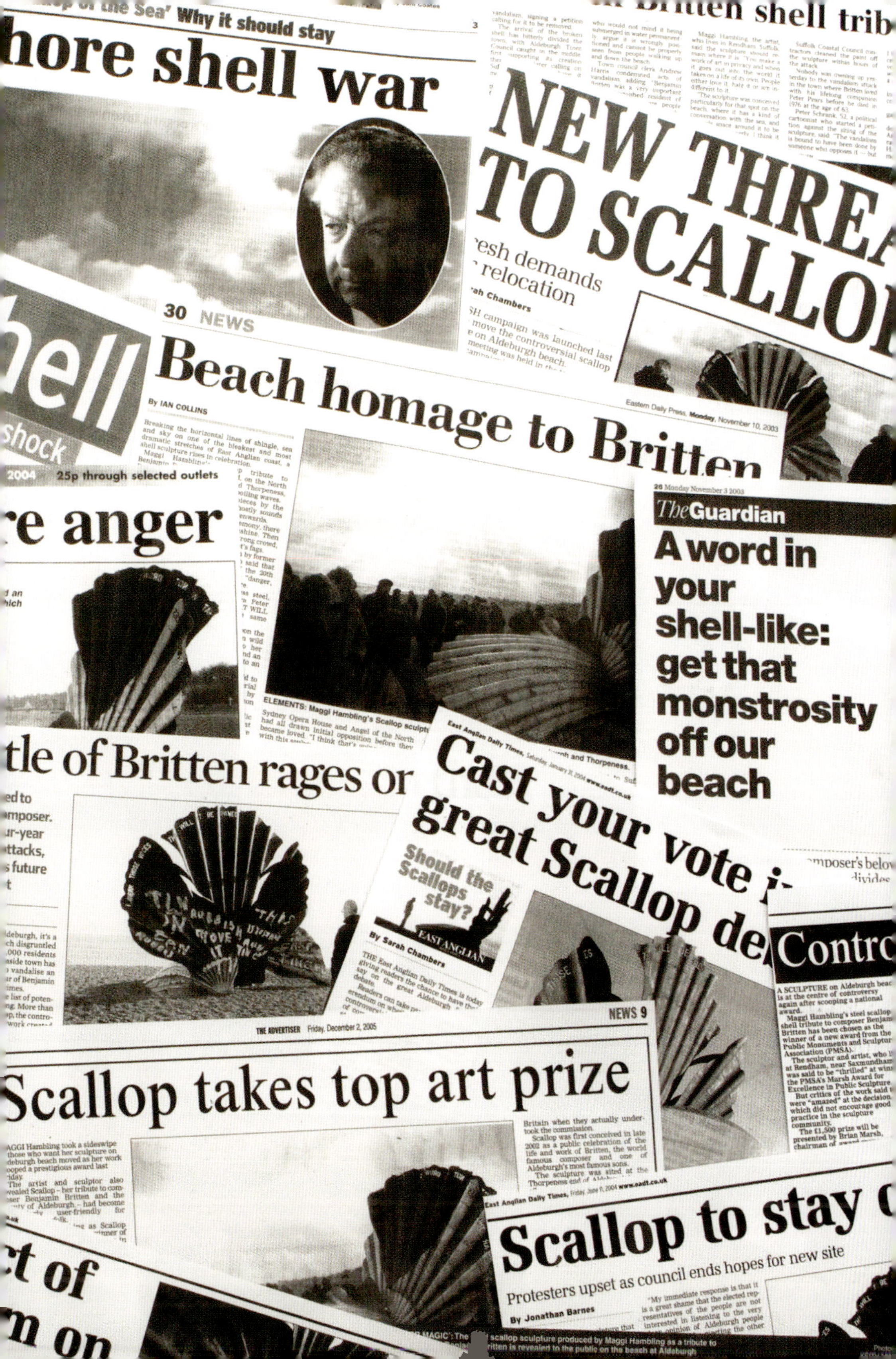
lop of the Sea' Why it should stay
hore shell war
NEW THREA
TO SCALLO
resh demands
relocation
Eastern Daily Press, Monday, November 10, 2003
Britten shell trib
30 NEWS
hell
shock
2004   25p through selected outlets
Beach homage to Britten
By IAN COLLINS
ELEMENTS: Maggi Hambling's Scallop sculpture
26 Monday November 3 2003
The Guardian
A word in
your
shell-like:
get that
monstrosity
off our
beach
re anger
tle of Britten rages on
Cast your vote i
great Scallop de
Should the
Scallops
stay?
By Sarah Chambers
EAST ANGLIAN
THE ADVERTISER Friday, December 2, 2005
NEWS 9
Contro
A SCULPTURE on Aldeburgh bea
Scallop takes top art prize
East Anglian Daily Times, Friday, June 8, 2004 www.eadt.co.uk
Scallop to stay
Protesters upset as council ends hopes for new site
By Jonathan Barnes

The voices of the people

The ferocity of the opposition to *Scallop* came as a complete shock. It never occurred to me that this sculpture, which was made with great love, and by the Peggs with such skill and craftsmanship, would not be received as it was offered, as a gift to the people of Aldeburgh to celebrate their greatest son. Petitions were drawn up, letters sent to newspapers, graffiti appeared on the sculpture. A small self-appointed committee grandly calling itself the Voices of the People of Aldeburgh launched a campaign, suggesting seven other sites where *Scallop* might be better accommodated, one of them in the car park at the Slaughden end of the town, next to the public lavatories. I found it incredible. The fact is that from its inception *Scallop* was created for the exact spot on which she now stands

Just over a month after *Scallop* had been installed the news came that she had been sprayed with graffiti. It said, "HAPPY CHRISTMAS. TIN CAN. MOVE IT." I was appalled and terribly hurt. I had given what I considered my most beautiful work to date. I felt for *Scallop* being abused. For all her size, I felt her vulnerability. You make a piece of work, and then it has a life of its own out in the world. I could no more defend *Scallop* against the graffiti sprayers than I could defend a ship against a storm. She was on her own.

I have had a long time to think about why a piece of sculpture might arouse such strong emotion—both for and against. Unlike a painting, sculpture shares your air, your ground, your space. It is always a confrontation, a three-dimensional invasion. Paintings,

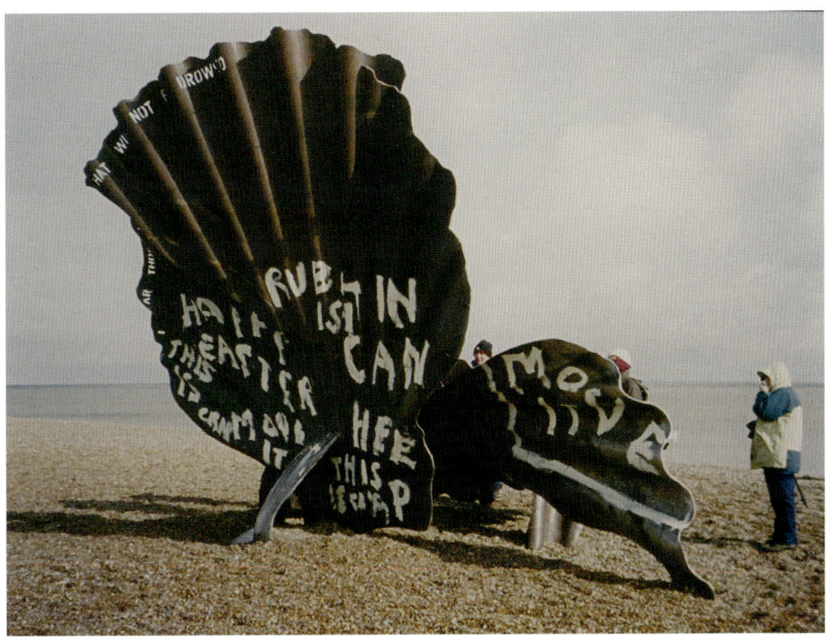

One of the graffiti attacks

safely on the wall, create their own interior space, which you can choose to enter or not. But there is the sculpture, stubbornly refusing to move.

The objectors have been loud but I don't believe they outnumber those who love *Scallop*. Some years ago the *East Anglian* invited its readers to vote for or against. That was quite a nerve-wracking period. But the result was more than three-to-one in favour. I suspect that now, with visitors from far and wide, the majority may be a good deal larger.

There is also the fact that any work of art that has a bit of life to it is bound to be controversial. And there is a history of people taking against public works of art who later love them. The Eiffel Tower was also at first hated by Parisians, and now it's the emblem of Paris. Certainly there are some who believe that if there were a serious attempt to move *Scallop*, to Birmingham, say, there'd be a pretty ferocious hue and cry of ownership.

If someone asked me by which of my works I would most like to be remembered, *Scallop*, so far, would be high on the list. It is great that there have been weddings there, and one or two funerals. Lovers have made love beneath her, children relish climbing all over her, and solitary walkers can find somewhere for contemplation.

I had an inspiration, and it still seems to me miraculous that it became a reality. It may be that her natural, organic shape touches something in people. I wanted to make

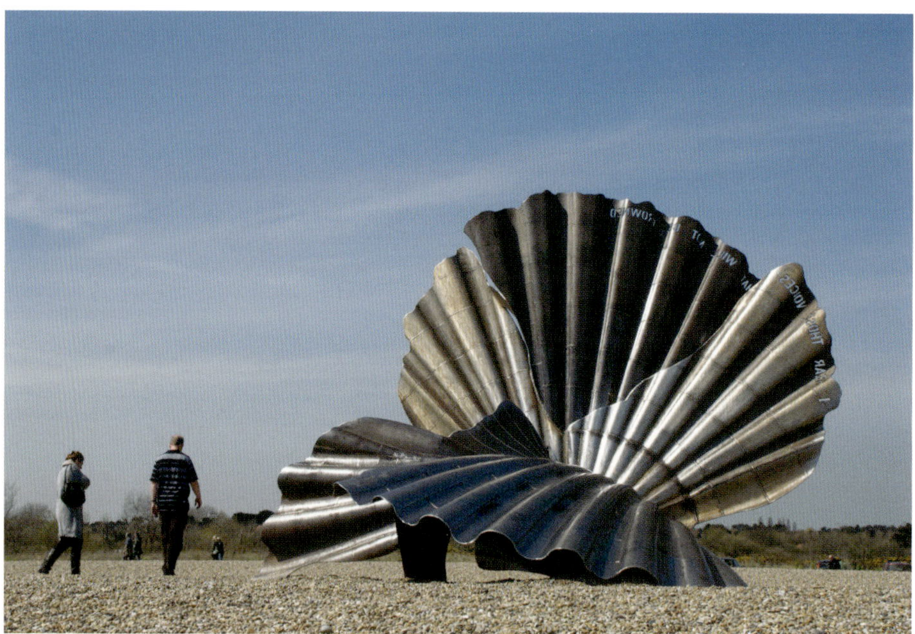

Scallop facing out to sea

a sculpture which amidst the rush and crush of life would afford quiet. Art, if it's any good, provides somewhere for the spirit to experience the sense of life and death simultaneously, coexisting together.

I was at *Scallop* one day doing an interview and a woman was standing a short way away. She was crying. I approached and asked her whether she was alright. She said, "Yes, yes, I'm fine. I come here three or four times a year to look at this and I think it's so beautiful that I cry every time."

At the height of the *Scallop* controversy I remember stopping off one morning on my way to the sea at one of the fishing huts in Aldeburgh. The fisherman was a particular friend from whom I often bought fish, though we rarely exchanged more than a couple of words. That morning I asked, "What do you think about *Scallop*? Do you think she's going to stay there?"

"Only one thing," he said in his true Suffolk voice, "only one thing will get rid of it."

"Oh," I said. "What's that?"

"Davy Jones," he replied, with a twinkle in his eye.

That's OK by me. Nothing I can do about that. If she has to disappear under the sea like Dunwich Church or Peter Grimes' village of Slaughden, so be it. And the way our coast is shifting, that could be sooner rather than later.

The sea endures

My obsession with painting the North Sea remains, and that, over time, has led to monoprints, etchings and new sea sculpture. I don't know why I suddenly decided to make a maquette of a rearing wave (p.60). But that sculpture is now a reality in bronze in a private landscape here in east Suffolk.

Early each morning I go the sea and draw. I identify with the shore, while the sea, like time, causes the inevitable erosion. It's a conversation with death each morning, or rather one between life and death. I wrote a poem entitled *You are the sea* (p.61).

I feel in these new sea paintings and bronzes that many phases of my work have come together. They refer back to my series of *Suffolk Sunrises* of the 1980s, of the *Laugh Paintings* in the 1990s, and to the earlier portraits of *Lett laughing, Tory laughing*. Aeschylus likened waves breaking to "unnumberable laughterings", and if you listen, you can hear them.

Over the years the paintings have increased in scale. The artist Penny Colman encouraged me in that—she also suggested that, whereas I had originally visualized the words "I hear those voices that will not be drowned" reading across the peak of the standing shell, they should instead begin lower down on the left-hand side as one looks at *Scallop* towards the sea, so that the words take the eye naturally up to the top of the sculpture, and on to the sky.

These large paintings are the freest things I've yet managed to make. Andrew

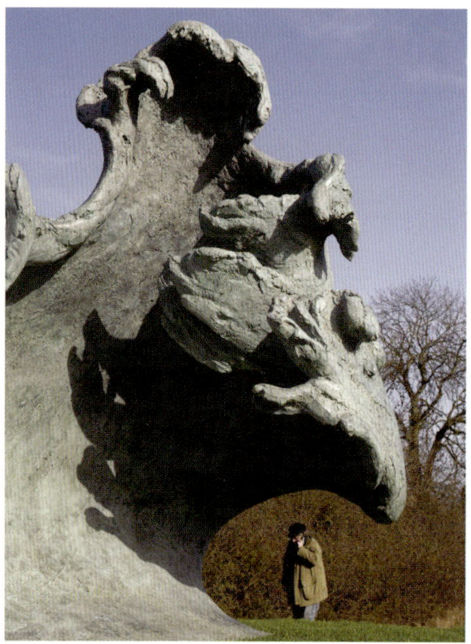

Rearing Wave (detail) 2009
bronze: height 3.5m, length 4.5m, depth 2.2m
private collection, Suffolk

Clarke of the *East Anglian* said when he came to see them, "If you do a portrait of, say, Stephen Fry, the first thing that comes to mind is, 'Oh yes, that's Stephen Fry. It's a person first before it's a painting. But in these, there's nothing between me and the sea that you paint." That's encouraging. It is precisely what I try to achieve.

After the bronze sculpture *Rearing Wave*, I made a 4m high, steel weather vane: *The Brixton Heron*, with the Peggs, deriving from a 1993 etching. It rises from the top of the classic 1920s Prince and Dex building close to the Ritzy Cinema in south London.

For me a vital part of a sculpture's integrity is its situation. Oscar Wilde still talking, laughing and smoking in a busy London street, a heron perching on a Brixton roof, a wave rearing up from a grass mound, a bird hovering above an altar, a scallop breaking out of Suffolk shingle.

you are the sea

I am the shifting shingle
you approach with stealth

Hot in the dark moons of your curves
I am tossed, lost, displaced

with greedy lovers' tongues and lips
you suck me in and in again

we rise together, we rise together
then float safe on liquid breasts

until the dance begins again
and you thrust deep

and my resistance is low
dissolve, dissolve,

no defence against your relentless advance
I am but a ghost of the shore

dispersed in you

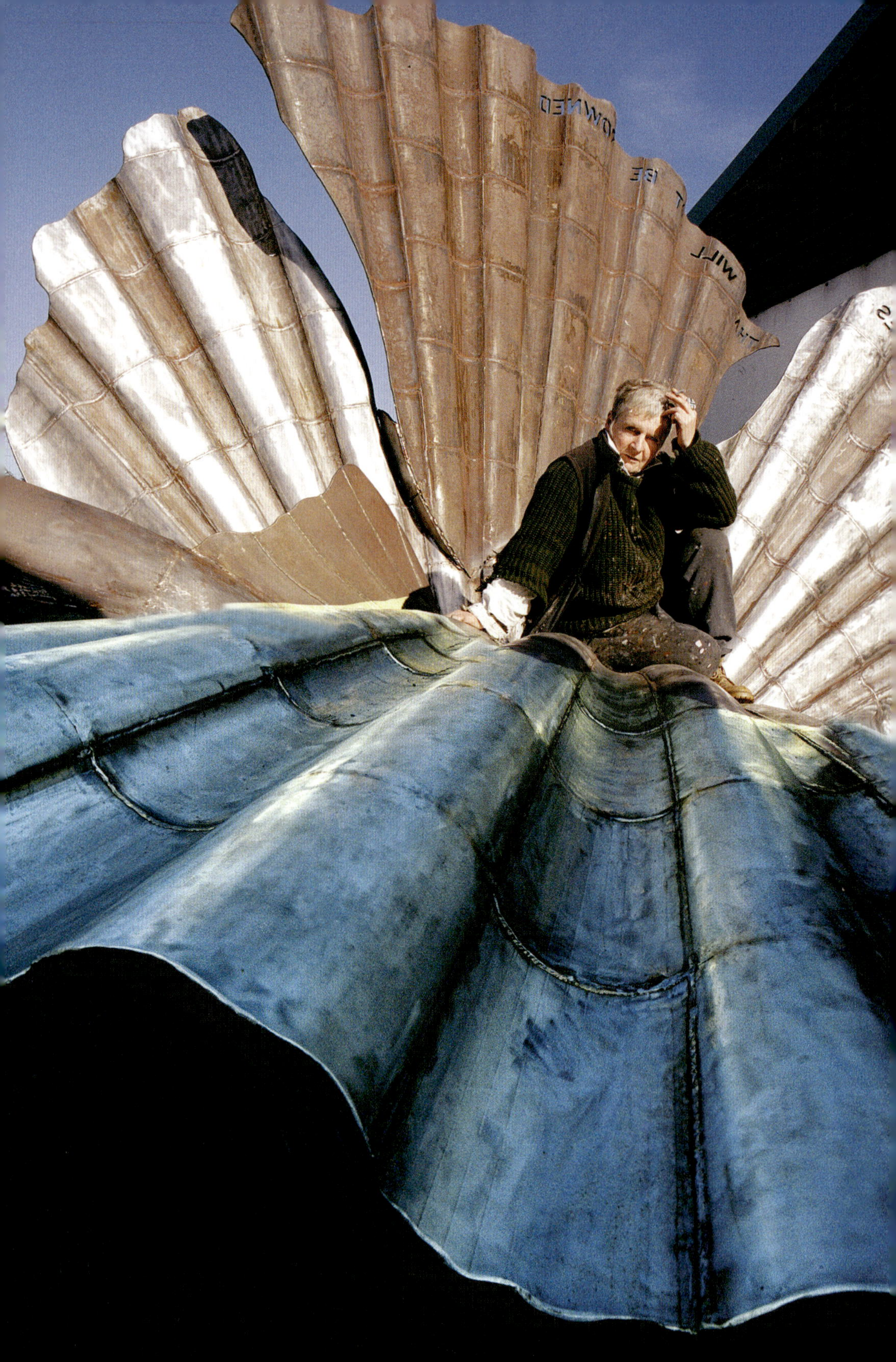
WILL
BE
DROWNED

Other voices

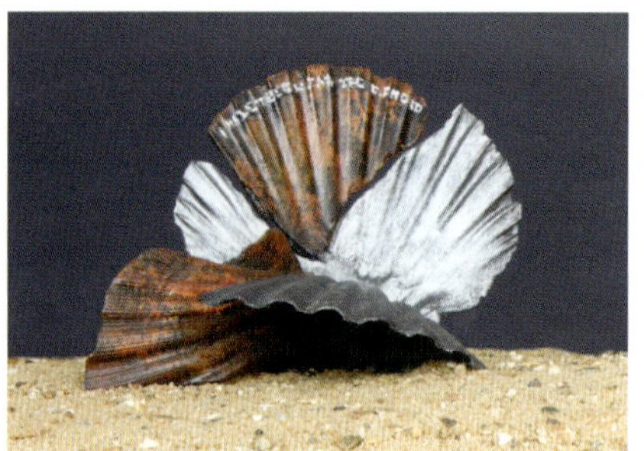

Scallop maquette, 2002
shell, sand and cardboard

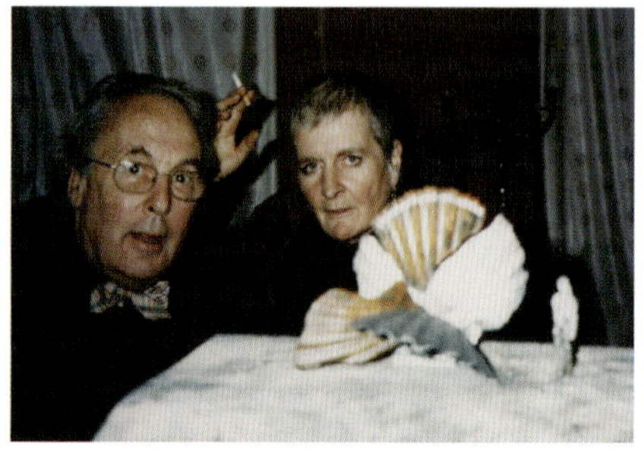

Nic Hill and MH with maquette
at Great Glemham House, 2002

Simon Loftus - *Southwold-based writer and former Chairman, Adnams*

I'd only met Maggi once, about a year beforehand, so when she contacted me about the *Scallop*, it came out of the blue. She just rang me up and said would I help. I agreed to meet and she showed me the maquette—this tiny, tiny model, made literally of broken scallop shells glued together. It was a bit of an act of faith to visualise it on the beach.

Maggi was under the illusion that I would have access to enormous sums of money, either personally or through my supposedly rich acquaintances, and thought that I'd be able to fundraise for this thing. None of that was true, as I told her straight away, but what I really could do, because I knew how it worked, was to help with the planning process and the whole business of getting planning permission, which was likely to be fantastically complicated. I knew the people and I knew the routes through the process.

It was obviously going to be difficult because, first of all, sticking a sculpture on Aldeburgh beach was bound to be controversial—whatever the sculpture. Second, I knew that there had been resistance in Aldeburgh for decades to any sort of memorial to Britten. There had always been a very ambiguous relationship between a large number of townspeople and the Aldeburgh Festival—and indeed with Britten personally. One of the things behind all that was homophobia—and also a lot of ill-feeling towards Britten's pacifism during the war. So there was bound to be a great deal of opposition to this sculpture, and I knew also that Aldeburgh was the sort of place where, if people got angry, they would tend to be quite persistently angry.

Then there were going to be issues to do with the natural environment—putting this sculpture on a shingle bank where a lot of plants were growing, natural shingle plants which were highly regarded by English Nature. So environmental issues, English Heritage issues, English Nature, everyone was going to want to have their say and get involved. It was going to be a complicated process, but I volunteered to help because I knew a lot of these people through my day job. I was Chairman of Adnams at the time and we had quite a lot of contact with the planning officers and with English Heritage—over pub alterations and the like—and I'd built up reasonably straightforward relationships with them.

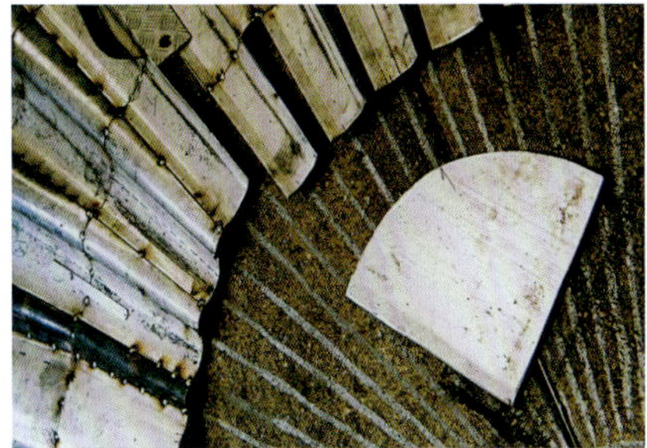 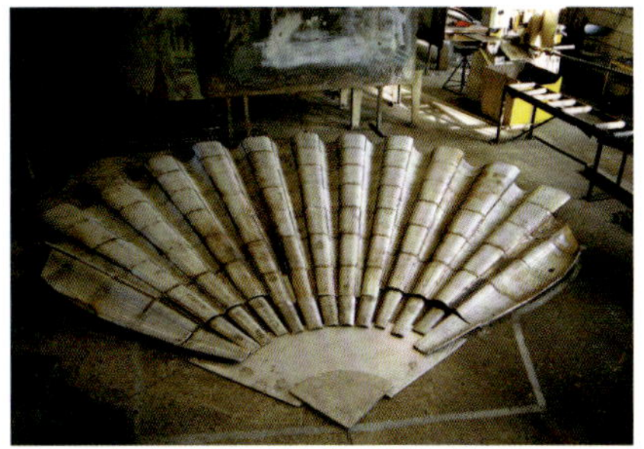

Scallop takes shape at the Peggs' workshop

But one of the things I said to Maggi right from the start was that Adnams as an organisation could not be involved. It would have been inappropriate of me to drag a public company of which I was Chairman into support for this project. As it later transpired we needed charitable status in order to reclaim Gift Aid on donations from private individuals to the *Scallop* appeal. It would have been very expensive to set up a separate charity, but Adnams as it happened had established a charitable trust which had a pretty wide scope to do things locally. So the trustees of the Adnams Charity agreed to open a separate account to receive the monies that Maggi and others raised for this sculpture, and thereby reclaim the tax.

The Charity itself did not give a penny to the project, in order to avoid the inevitable politics. This proved a wise move because the leader of the so-called Voices of the People barged his way into the Adnams Annual General Meeting one year and stood up at question time and started ranting and raving about Adnams and me having given financial and other support for the sculpture and wasn't it a waste of shareholders' money—so it was just as well that I was able to say to him that not a single penny had been spent by Adnams, either directly or through its charitable trust.

But I did have a network of contacts and that was quite useful. I've always talked to the planners on the basis that they're not monsters but have a life which is governed by regulations of various sorts—and that it's in both our interests to sit down together and try to work out solutions rather than assume there is going to be conflict. That worked quite well in this context, and in fact there were some very helpful people within Suffolk Coastal District Council who were supportive of the scheme. There was a councillor called Maggy Wilson who was a great ally, right from the start. She and Maggi Hambling and I would have regular meetings with Council officers to try to move the project forward. Philip Ridley, the Head of Planning, understood the importance of the project as did John Davies, who helped a great deal in the negotiations with English Nature—while Kevin Gosling (who now works for the Britten-Pears Foundation) was particularly good at framing applications to the various grant-giving bodies, once planning permission was granted. And Ray Herring, as Leader, proved wonderfully strong when the controversy was at its height.

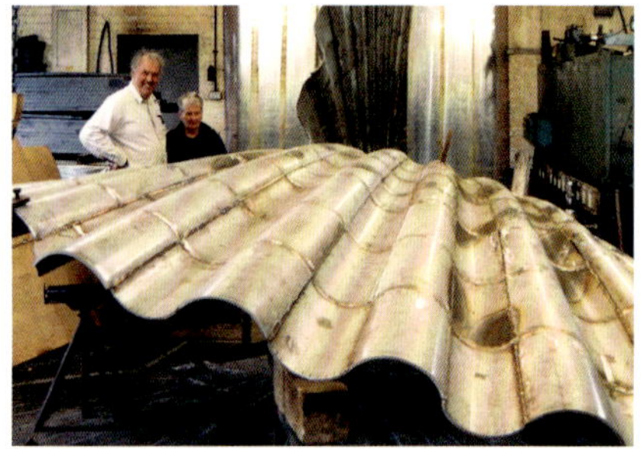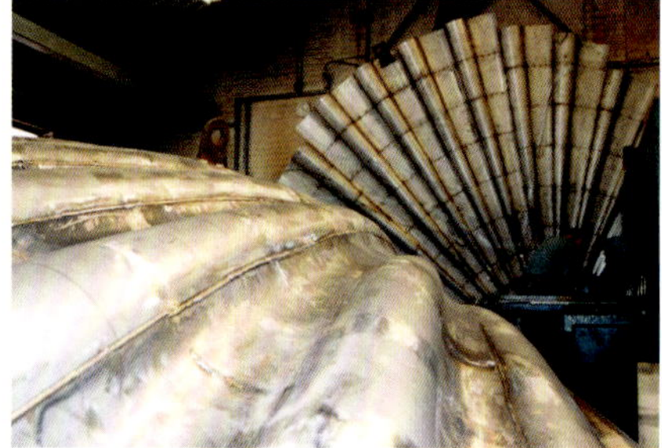

Sam and MH as *Scallop* progresses

English Nature and English Heritage were much harder to deal with, and we had a lot of very difficult meetings with them. One of the other key issues which concerned English Nature, and indeed Suffolk Coastal District Council, was that a big, concrete base for this sculpture might itself cause movement and instability in the shingle bank and would almost certainly cause considerable disruption to the natural processes which supported the various vegetations. But I managed to find an engineer, Andrew Hawes, who knew everything there was to be known about shingle banks on this particular stretch of coastline. He knew which were stable and which were not, and he established that the bank where we eventually sited the sculpture had not moved for 400 years—and that despite its apparent fragility, it wasn't going to move. He also knew how to design an anchorage for the sculpture which did not involve any concrete. What he came up with was a very interesting design which was basically a series of metal struts going down from the base of sculpture to a large metal tray buried in the shingle, and this tin tray is simply held in place by the weight of the shingle itself. It's a very elegant structure which uses the beach to anchor the sculpture.

It was then, when we'd got planning permission, that the real controversy started, with the opponents of the *Scallop* expressing their views in the most vitriolic ways. My role then was to muzzle Maggi. With all the journalists and television people coming along and trying to stir up controversy by quoting the opposition, her instinct was naturally to explode with fury and passion in talking to them. She'd want to return fire with fire. But I knew that our best strategy was to stay calm, and let the storm pass. "Come on, Maggi", I'd say, "we don't do controversy. We're the goodies, not the baddies."

There was one other thing that was important. Once the sculpture had been made and was in situ, what was going to happen to it? What would happen to the ongoing ownership of *Scallop* in terms of insurance, public liability, maintenance in the event of people spraying it as they did? So I was clear from a very early stage that the right thing to do was to give it to Suffolk Coastal District Council. I got a big legal agreement drawn up by their solicitors. So now we have no problems about the future and it also means that they are proud of it—the *Scallop* is theirs.

But I have to say that at the beginning of the whole project I felt somewhat uncertain

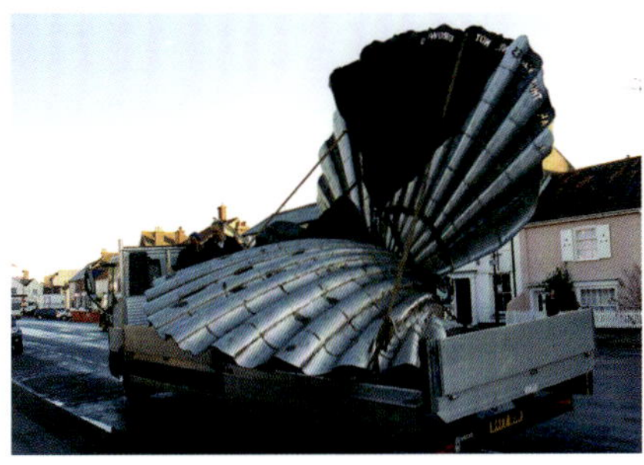

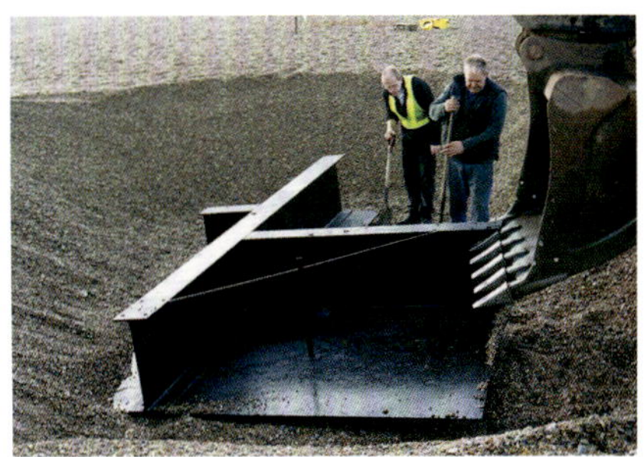

Early morning, Aldeburgh High Street
6th November 2003

The foundation tray

about the sculpture itself. It was difficult to be really sure that this small thing, the maquette made out of scallop shells, was going to work at the scale and magnification Maggi envisaged for it. It was very hard to tell. But there was something about it I liked, and I certainly liked Maggi and thought that she was a real artist—she wasn't a fake and she wasn't producing something that was simply pretty. So much public sculpture is rubbish, but this was the real thing. Whether you liked it or not it was a proper work of art.

What really convinced me and got me enthusiastic was when we started working with the Peggs. Maggi was determined right from the start that the Peggs were the people who were going to make this. They'd been metal-bashers in Aldeburgh for generations and she wanted it to be made locally. As soon as she took me to their yard to show me the *Scallop* in progress, I realised the thing was going to work. They are the most wonderful people and the whole way that they approached the making of the sculpture was so exciting. You suddenly realised this was not going to be some sort of sleekly cast piece of art; this was really going to be made properly. I remember Maggi telling me that at the first proper meeting where the fabrication was discussed she showed this tiny maquette to Sam and Dennis and said,"I want one like this but 38 times the size". Anywhere else you'd expect some sort of sophisticated way of computerising the design, digitalising it, so that they could then blow it up and make scale drawings. That didn't happen here at all, they cleared a space in the workshop and Dennis or Sam started drawing in chalk on the floor, the shapes of the shell. And then they started making it. It was made as they worked, that was the great thing about it. Maggi would go along and work with them, saying that she wanted it more polished here or roughened up a bit there, and all the shapes and the way they were welded together started to feel terrific. That gave me complete confidence.

The real vindication came once it was there on the beach. One of the things that people who opposed it often said was not,'We hate it, you're philistines'but'This may be a wonderful work of art but it shouldn't be here'. They used the idea that it could be moved to another site as a means of muddling the debate. But the *Scallop* is entirely site-specific; it absolutely had to be where it is. It needs to be on a stretch of beach

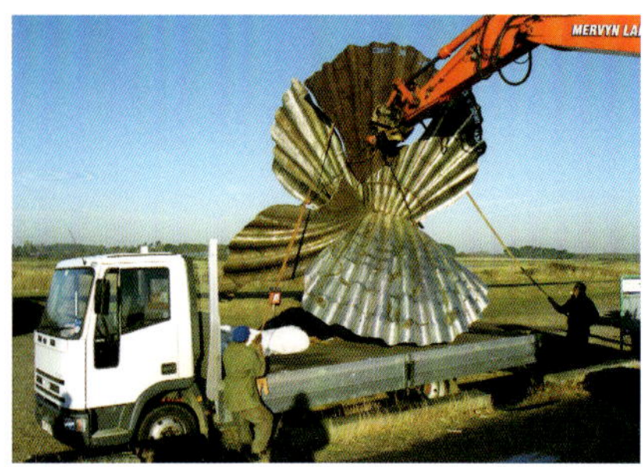

Unloading at the beach site

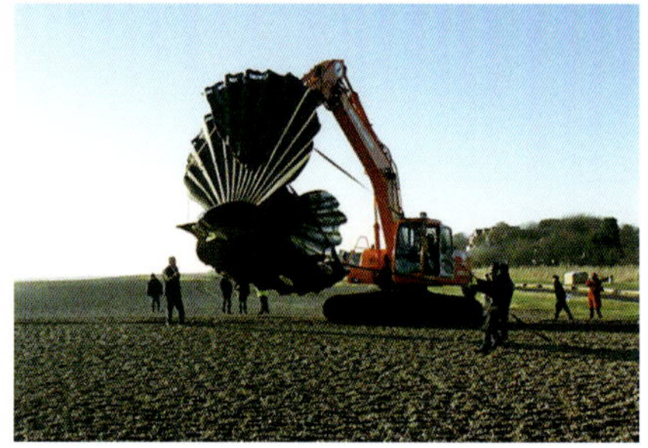

Installation, Aldeburgh beach, 6th November 2003

where it's not too much surrounded by other things, where you feel a sense of wind and space and weather around it. It's got to relate directly to the shingle, it mustn't sit on a plinth. There were proposals to put it in the car park, on tarmac and concrete. It's inconceivable that this sculpture could have worked in those kinds of environment.

When I really thought, this is it, fantastic, was when it had been installed where it is, there, on the beach, shingle all around it, waves and weather and foul weather—it's especially terrific in foul weather. I helped Maggi and various others to cover it in a white fleece before the unveiling ceremony a few days later, and we were battling against high winds trying to rip this fleece off it, and then we really began to realise what a wonderful thing it was. Maggi talks about couples going to the shell and making love underneath it, under the curve of the shell, children climbing all over it and dogs peeing on it. Here's a thing to be used properly by people and not some sort of distant work of art you are not allowed to touch or scratch. Maggi got a bit grumpy when they started spraying slogans on it, but in fact it is made of stainless steel, it's a rough thing, it's strong, so it didn't really matter very much. Those things can be cleaned off and it stands there impervious to all that rubbish. That's what is great about it.

Those who were hostile always were a minority. I know they called themselves the Voices of the People but that simply wasn't true. Such polls as were taken showed that they were a minority, a relatively small minority. At one point they presented Suffolk Coastal District Council with a petition signed by 800 people saying that the *Scallop* should be taken away. More than half those people were not Aldeburgh people. Within three days Suffolk Coastal District Council had a petition signed by 600 people saying it should stay where it was. That petition would have been signed by many more if there had been more time. The opponents were always a minority but they were very, very determined.

One of the great things about this project is that everyone involved was local. Maggi is local and the sculpture was made by the Peggs. Andrew Hawes, who designed the foundations, is also local. It's not some imported work of art dumped thoughtlessly on Aldeburgh beach, which is the way it's often spoken about by its opponents. It's a completely, wonderfully indigenous thing. That is what people will feel and notice about

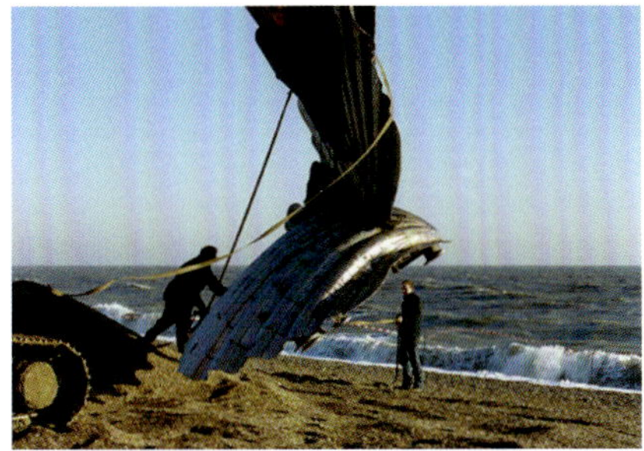 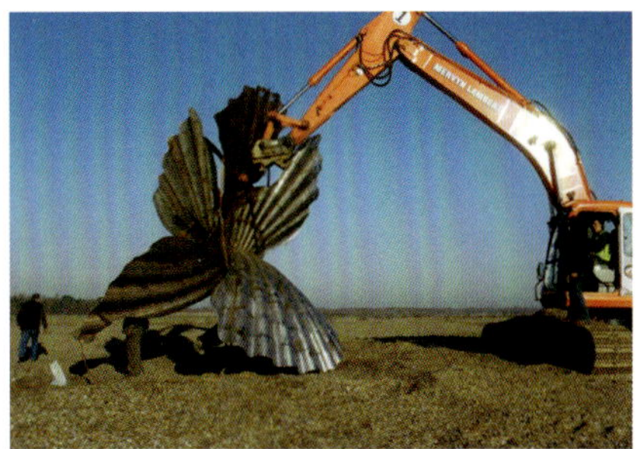

Lowering *Scallop* on to her foundations

it in the long term. Especially now, as the controversy has more or less died away. The fact of the matter is that every shop in Aldeburgh has got mugs and postcards and fridge magnets showing the *Scallop*. It's been of enormous economic benefit to Aldeburgh.

There is this bizarre feeling, which was very well expressed by one of the journalists who wrote about the sculpture—the assumption that there's an intrinsic opposition between unsullied nature and works of art, that you can't put a sculpture into nature without spoiling its 'naturalness'. This proposition begs all sorts of questions, but as far as I'm concerned the prime question that it raises is the notion of unsullied nature. Almost all the landscape we have has been shaped in one way or another by human activity, historically and currently.

If you walk down the beach from Aldeburgh towards the *Scallop*, what you see in the distance is the great dome and block of Sizewell nuclear power station, which I feel looks pretty terrific, irrespective of what you think about nuclear power. That's a strong part of the landscape. But on the left as you go northwards out of Aldeburgh towards Thorpeness is what is probably the ugliest block of flats built within 50 miles from here. God knows how it got planning permission. It's mind-bogglingly ugly. You can't go for a walk down that beach without being completely shocked and horrified by that. Then you've got this relatively tiny object sitting on the beach which, if it wasn't a sculpture could be a bit of wrecked boat, which people would think was rather romantic. It's not the thing itself—it's what people project onto it from their own minds and their own prejudices.

When I see the *Scallop* now I'm very happy. Almost always when you're passing you see people sitting on it, climbing, photographing it, enjoying it in various ways. Even in the worst weather there's always somebody there. I love it. But the big thing I got out of this personally was that I got to know Maggi, and I absolutely adore Maggi. She can sometimes seem a monster but she's the most lovable person. I'm flattered that she now calls me brother. I feel very honoured.

And despite the madness of it all, the frustrations, it was great fun, those absurd battles.

Dennis Pegg - *JT Pegg & Sons, Engineers, Aldeburgh*

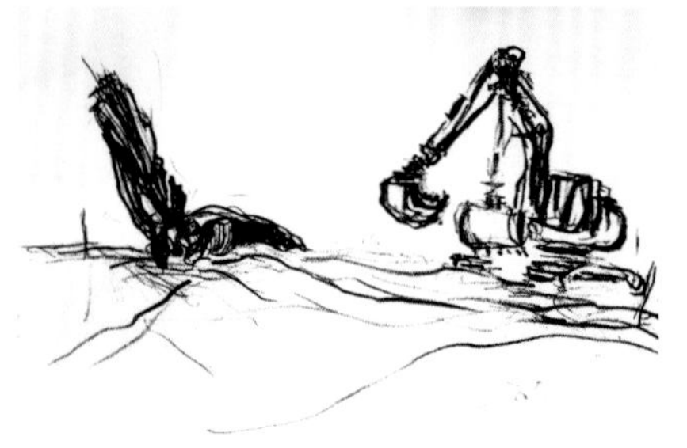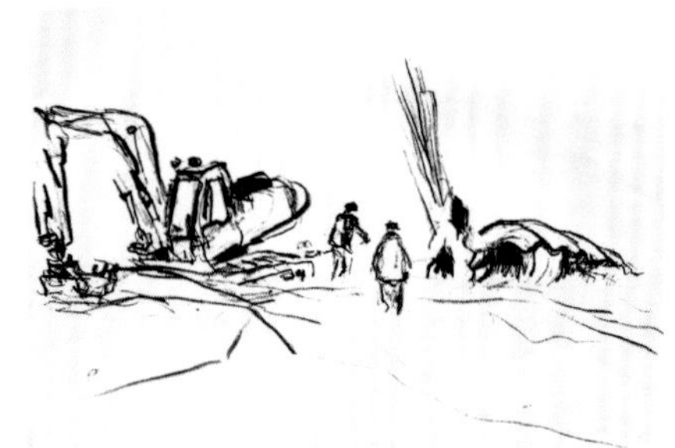

Three sketchbook drawings of the installation, Aldeburgh beach, 6/7th November 2003, Jason Gathorne-Hardy

I joined my dad here in 1997, when I was 20. I'd been working here on and off since I was 15, weekends and holidays.

When Maggi first came in what she wanted was a seat with a shell behind it, completely different to what it became. We said yes, we could do it, but as with a lot of things that come through the door you don't know whether they will materialize or not. A couple of visits later she came back with the actual maquette and gave us the go-ahead.

There were no drawings, all we had was the maquette, and we'd never been asked to do anything like this before. We had some scallop shells and we started scaling off, drew a few things off on the floor in the workshop. Dad's engineering experience told him that 10mm stainless steel was what it wanted to be. At first Father took very much the leading role as he had all those years' experience. We started off with the dished end, with fabricated spines that you can now see on the base as you walk towards the *Scallop*, similar to a saucer but with a very smooth radius. We had one of them, which was stainless, and we laid it on the floor and tilted it back until we thought it was right, did a few cuts here and there to lose the bottom edge of it, and that's how we started building it.

The whole process took seven months. One of the biggest problems was the amount of curving. There's not a straight line anywhere. You're trying to taper the fins, which go away from you. But they're also curved the other way, there's a lot of shape involved, cutting bits here and there and putting them together, like a jigsaw. We put it through the bender. There were welding issues as well, we had to get the welding right because there were so many different positions that needed welding together. And there was a lot of vertical welding that had to be done.

We could see it all happening, it was a bit like when you build a house, it just gradually gets bigger. But then we had to finish it outside the workshop because it was too big. We made two shells, and at the end they had to be put together. At that point it was put by the crane and the forklift on to our lorry and we drove it down the road, very slowly, with Father walking ahead with a pole to keep the electricity and telephone wires out of the way. We did it early in the morning, but there were some people in the high street poking their heads around the side of the door. There were a few jeers and a few nice comments.

Now we feel very proud of it from an engineering point of view. It won the best public

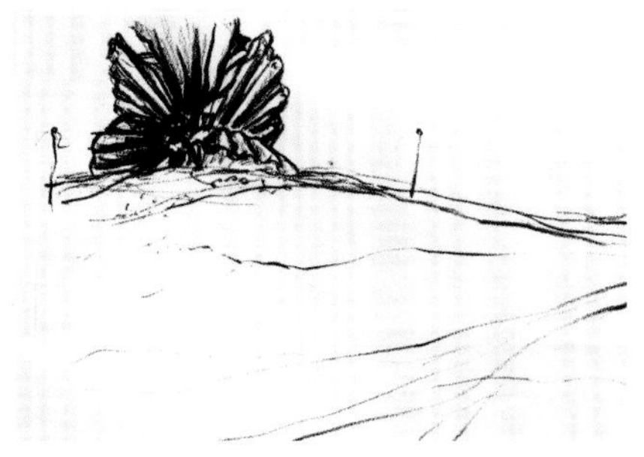

sculpture in Britain award, the Marsh Award, and that also was quite a day. We didn't realise how big an event it was going to be until we got there, journalists interviewing you, lots of interviews and people milling about.

Once Father and I were on the underground in London and there was an advertisement for East Anglia and the *Scallop* was what they used, and you thought, blimey, that's quite a big thing…They must be quite proud of it if they use it to advertise Suffolk and East Anglia.

Now when I go past the *Scallop*, when I come into Aldeburgh on the Leiston-Aldeburgh road you can see it across the marshes, and every time I come into work I glance at it, check that it's still there. I think later on in life it will become more important to me. I've got my first child due in seven weeks' time so I hope he or she will say, "My Dad made that."

Maggy Wilson - *Former Cabinet Member for Culture and the Arts, Suffolk Coastal District Council*
I was on Suffolk Coastal District Council—I was the Cabinet Member for Culture and the Arts—when I first came across Maggi Hambling's idea for the *Scallop*. It put me right in the hot seat, really.

I knew Maggi's painting and admired it. And I was keen on a tribute to Benjamin Britten because I thought it was very fitting. The town council had earlier turned down the idea of a statue. We already had a window in the Anglican Church and they thought that was enough. In Aldeburgh there are people who always complain about everything, whatever it is.

I think it was after it had actually been installed on the beach that the objections began. There may have been a hundred people who were against it but to call themselves the Voices of the People of Aldeburgh was rubbish. Fortunately the District Council didn't pay much attention to it. Now I still find it absolutely beautiful. I always have. And I think it's absolutely right in the position it's in. It rises from the beach, and it's in communication with the sea and the land. It just seems a perfect whole to me and perfectly appropriate as a tribute to Benjamin Britten, because of his relationship to the sea and to that place.

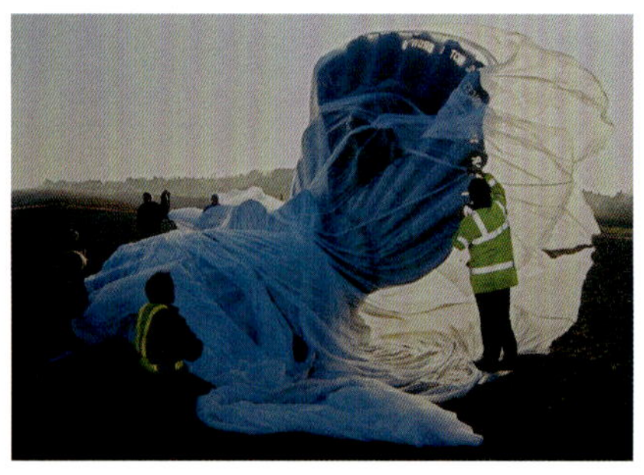

Attempting to cover *Scallop* with agricultural fleece

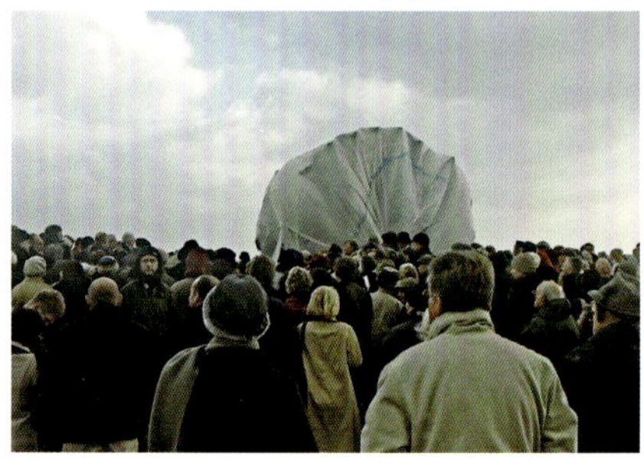

Just before mid-day, 8th November 2003

Jonathan Reekie - *Chief Executive, Aldeburgh Music*

Scallop would not have happened without Maggi's extraordinary determination to realize her vision. The two greatest challenges she faced were raising the money to fund the sculpture and getting permission to put it up. It was clear it ought to be positioned within Peter Grimes's landscape, but this is a landscape that is much protected and much loved.

I couldn't help with the fund raising but I could put Maggi in touch with the people she needed to consult about where the sculpture might go and how to get the necessary permissions.

When *Scallop* was finally installed on the beach, I walked towards it thinking how subtly it sat in the landscape from a distance only to find, when I got close, that it was bigger than I'd imagined. At the opening Maggi told me she thought it would be a good shelter for lovers. I agreed. It has become a shelter for everyone, and I always enjoy the ways in which people engage with it, particularly children, who clamber all over it.

But of course, *Scallop* was, and in some quarters remains, an object of hostility. With hindsight, there perhaps wasn't enough public consultation, or rather the right kind of consultation. The planning process is not very effective in this respect for sculpture, so there was never a proper feeling that this was something that the majority of the community wanted. Works of art rarely please everyone, but despite the controversy surrounding it, *Scallop* has already become an iconic image of this part of the Suffolk coast.

Is it a suitable tribute to Benjamin Britten? Britten would probably have liked the way it captures the sounds of the elements. It encourages you to listen.

Ray Herring - *Leader, Suffolk Coastal Distric Council*

I first became aware of the idea of the *Scallop* when, before Suffolk Coastal District Council dealt with it in planning terms, it was flagged up the year before as a project. At that time it looked as if it had a good measure of local support.

But for the sculpture to be placed on the beach required Suffolk Coastal Cabinet to make that decision. We looked at the likely impact it would have, the potential benefits as a piece of public art, and whether it would enhance the attraction of Aldeburgh. You realized that

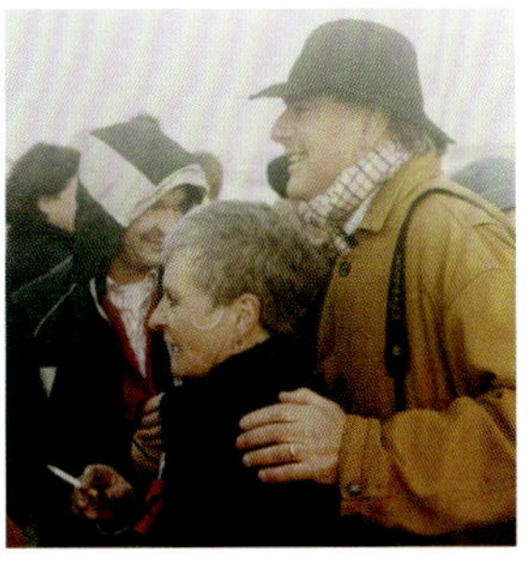

MH and Simon Loftus

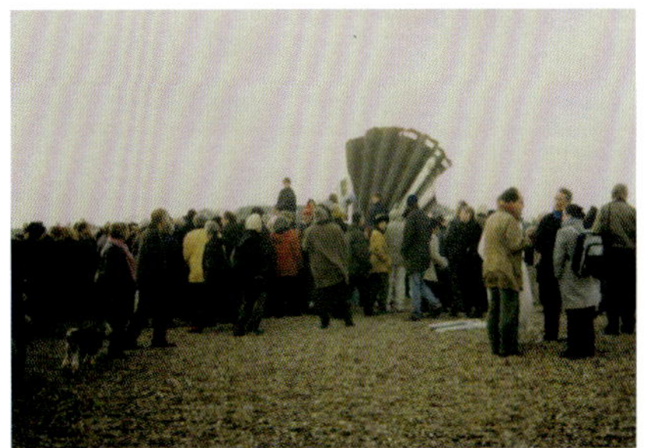

After the unveiling

with pieces of public art not everyone would be supportive, but at that time it looked as if, broadly, Aldeburgh and the surrounding areas were supportive.

But the consultation processes gave rise to quite a lot of objections from Aldeburgh. The town council had initially given it what appeared to be support, but under the pressure of the objectors the town council became more lukewarm.

But we went through the processes and we gave it permission. There was then an even greater furore among the objectors once the *Scallop* was actually put in place. A campaign group was set up with a view to getting it moved out of Aldeburgh. We held a review and looked at our decisions to make sure they were sound, but also, in response to what was a large number of objectors, we looked at possible alternative sites, within Aldeburgh but also outside the town, such as Snape Maltings. But in practice it turned out to be very difficult to find somewhere else for the *Scallop* to go.

The objectors then organised a public meeting in the Jubilee Hall. It was packed to the ceiling, and it seemed to me all those who were against the *Scallop* were there. On the stage were the campaign committee—The Voices of the People of Aldeburgh. I was invited to go along. I took an officer and a Council solicitor with me, and I was made to feel the heat of 400 people on my collar. It was uncomfortable, I have to say. But I did the best I could to explain the processes we had gone through, and the lack of alternative sites.

Yes, there were objectors. But I'm a local person and I had a number of local contacts, a number of people I know in Aldeburgh, in businesses there and residents, and very clearly there were also a lot of people who were very supportive of it. Among those I spoke to there was a very clear level of support, not just from those who support the arts in general but also from local people, people who were born and bred in Aldeburgh. When you have a planning application the supporters often don't come forward; it's always the objectors, and you've got to weigh that up. At the same time you could start to see the number of people who were coming to visit Aldeburgh and see the *Scallop,* and the trade that that was bringing in. From an early stage it was clear there were many benefits to the *Scallop.*

Then the *East Anglian Daily Times* did a survey. It came out heavily in favour of retaining the *Scallop* where it was. Together with the feedback from the arts community and the local community in general, and also taking into account the potential of attracting tourists to

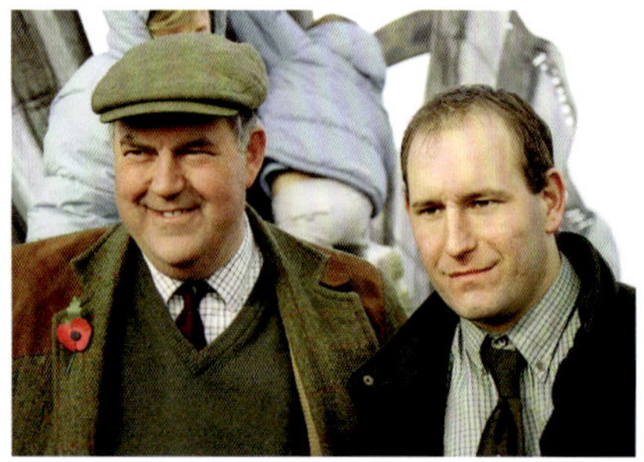

Sam and Dennis after the unveiling

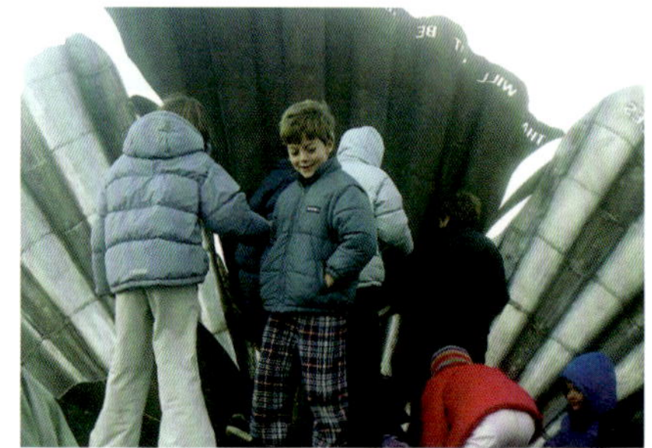

Testing the strength of the sculpture

Aldeburgh and supporting the local economy, Suffolk Coastal took the decision to keep the *Scallop* where it was. It was one of those situations where things were in the balance, and as Leader I did feel the weight of that decision on my shoulders.

Now, of course, the *Scallop* has proved to be phenomenally successful. The marvellous thing about it, from my point of view, is that families, and especially children, go and look at it and appreciate it. They jump all over it. It's a marvellous thing to have there.

Looking back, it's hard to understand what drove the hostility to the *Scallop*. You have a number of communities in Aldeburgh—the business community, the arts community, the local community, the retired—and of course from time to time there are issues that get raised, whether it's the church bells that ring too loudly on a Sunday or whether there are too many seagulls. So it's a very interesting place to live in, and you've got many influential people, some very successful people, who have come to retire in Aldeburgh, often with strong views.

That creates Aldeburgh's very interesting social environment. There's never a dull moment. So when you get something like the *Scallop*, which means change, hostility can snowball. But in all such things a politician has to weigh things up.

And I can understand how people felt. Aldeburgh is a very special place, both in terms of its natural and built environment and socially. Along with Southwold it sets a standard for the whole East Suffolk coast. It certainly helps us deliver quality tourism in the area. Part of that is retaining that environment. So I do understand where the objectors were coming from. I believe the *Scallop* enhances that environment, but I'm sure not everyone will agree with me on that.

I also believe, now, that it's a very appropriate monument to Benjamin Britten. I don't pretend to be knowledgeable about art. Music or visual art was not a big factor in my education, so it's been a learning curve for me as well. I'm basically a practical, local working farmer. But through the whole *Scallop* experience I've taken on board what the visual arts can do and what they can provide for our local economy. Initially I didn't necessarily understand it, but now I do, whether in terms of its engineering, the message it conveys or the location, the background of the North Sea. And I'm pleased to have played a small part in it being there.

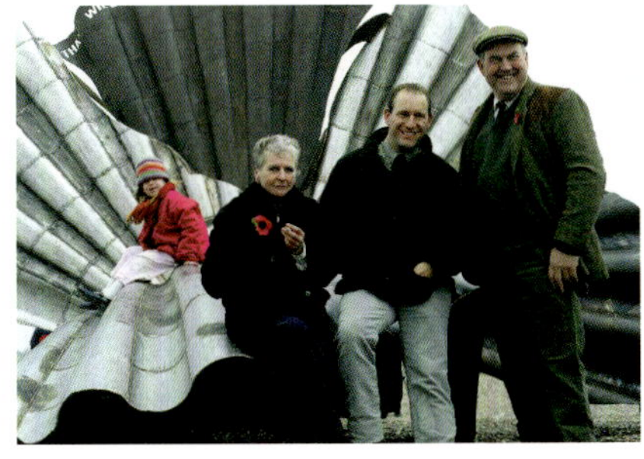

MH, Dennis and Sam

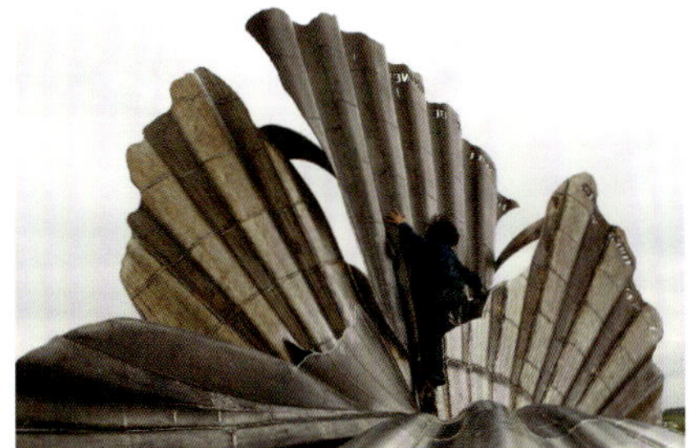

A young mountaineer

Sam Pegg - *J T Pegg & Sons, Engineers, Aldeburgh*

Peggs have been in Aldeburgh since 1912. We're fourth generation, and I'm certain we'd never been asked to do anything like this till Maggi came along with her shell.

We didn't know who she was at that time. Then she came back with the maquette. I didn't envisage how large it was going to be at that point, or how heavy a gauge material: 10mm stainless is how it finished up in, and stainless is a completely different cup of tea. We thought she might be just a little bit bonkers, but you find that with a lot of people in these parts.

Everything about the shell was on a taper, everything had got a curve. And no sooner did it curve one way than it had to curve back another way. So we thought about it and tried different ideas and we couldn't really come up with a solution, at the start anyway. Then we thought about how you build a house, one brick at a time. That was how we did it. We'd never done anything like it at that size or scale.

Size was definitely an issue. The bigger it gets the heavier it gets. It ended up weighing three and a half tons. Three and a half tons above ground and another three tons in the ground.

Why did some people not like it? Some people don't like change, especially down here in Aldeburgh. The location also gave some people an excuse for something to grumble about. I bet half the people who grumbled about the location never used the location at all. I remember the metal stakes and poles that were there before and nobody ever complained about them. They were just rusty bits of metal sticking out of the ground to show where the shingle fell away.

We don't go by there much nowadays but it's nice when we do. We slow down, and there's another coach-load of people and all the old biddies getting out and stomping up the beach to have a look at it. And all the kids clambering all over it. It's become a landmark now. A new generation of people will just take it for granted and enjoy it. The material it's made of means it's going to be there a long time.

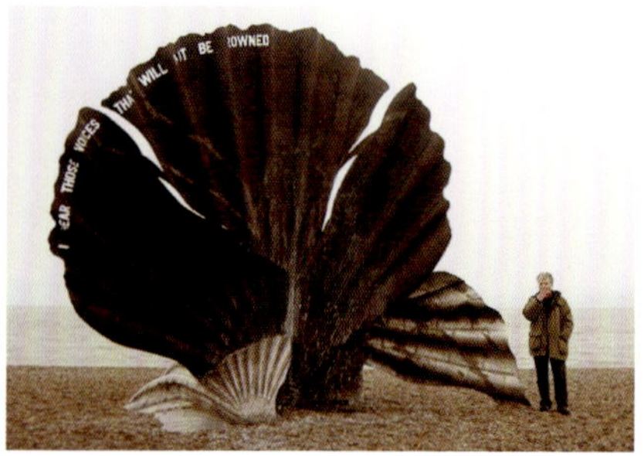

MH and *Scallop*

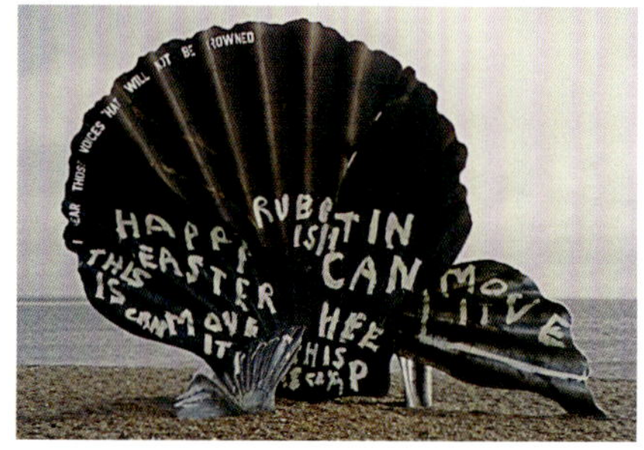

Graffiti, 2007

Scallop—A Survey *Jason Gathorne-Hardy, January 2004*

On the afternoon of 24th January 2004, I spent four hours interviewing visitors to the *Scallop* sculpture on Aldeburgh beach, asking their opinions both about the sculpture and the local debate about whether to move it or leave it where it was.

Members of the public were approached and asked if they would like to answer a series of questions about the *Scallop*. The survey was conducted independently of any petitions to move the sculpture or leave it where it was. Its sole purpose was to gather opinion and information from people visiting the sculpture and the beach. Interviewees were each asked a set of four questions:

— What do you think of the sculpture? Do you:
  a) like it?
  b) dislike it?
  c) have no opinion?
— There are local proposals to move the sculpture.
  Do you:
  a) agree?
  b) disagree?
  c)want to know why?
  d)have no opinion?
— Where are you from?
— Have you come especially to see the sculpture?

During the four-hour survey I approached 193 people. Of these, 191 agreed to be interviewed. Two local residents declined to be interviewed, on the basis that they disliked the sculpture and wanted it moved but did not want to answer any questions.

What do you think of the sculpture?

152 people said that they liked the sculpture Of these, 14 emphasised this as a very strong liking. Interviewees referred to or described the work in strong terms: "fantastic","gorgeous""beautiful","wonderful","love it","adore it","great piece of art in a wonderful situation","relates to the sea,"lot of hard work making it","great as a piece of work","enhances vistas in both directions","suits the beach","striking",

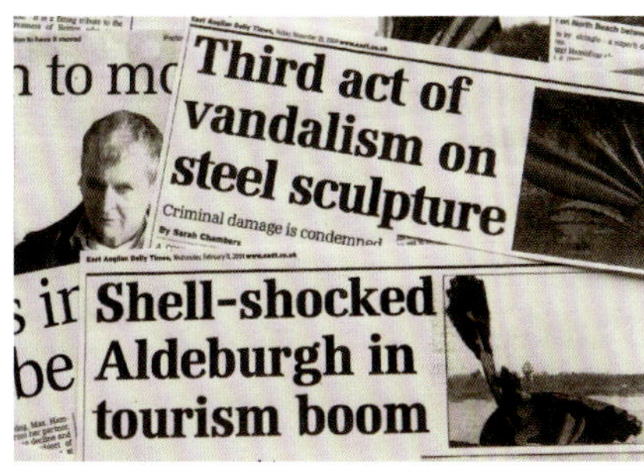

Newspaper reactions to *Scallop*

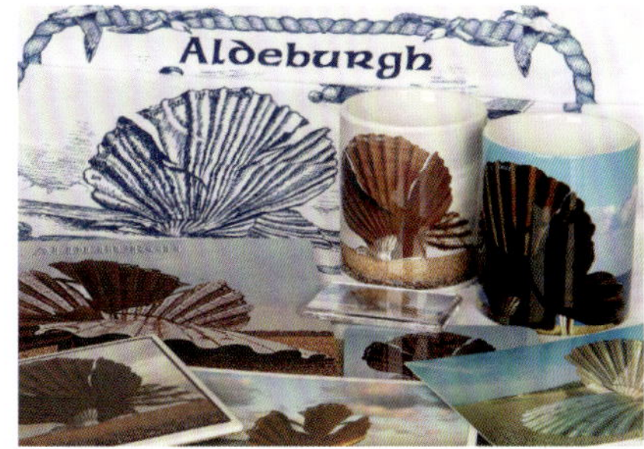

Aldeburgh merchandise, from mugs to mouse mats

"robust and played upon", "first class", "very exciting piece of sculpture", "draws people out of town", "decent art is always controversial", "it's talked about in Norwich".

Some interviewees who liked the sculpture added qualifying comments or reservations, e.g. certain aspects or angles looked better than others; "interesting but the wrong way round"; "looks strange at a distance but better as you get closer"; "weathering will improve it"; "looks better than Sizewell", "the best climbing frame I've ever seen"; "if it were moved it would be a great shame".

Fourteen people said that they disliked it; of these, four said they really disliked it. One described it as irrelevant; another asked how it had come to be placed on a heritage beach. Other comments included: "well made but not relevant"; "it's a work of art but out of place", "unwanted", "waste of money".

There are local proposals to move it. Do you agree?

Thirty-three people agreed with the local campaign to move the sculpture. Some respondents felt that the present site did not do the sculpture justice; others felt it did not suit the beach at this particular location; or that it would be better located nearer the town. Others said it would look better further away from the town. Some suggestions for alternative destinations included: 30 yards closer to the car park; further away from the town; closer to the town; Fort Green; the Moot Hall; in front of Benjamin Britten's house; Aldeburgh churchyard, the town roundabout; Snape Maltings; on a hill (like the Angel of the North); the river wall (where the houseboat Iona used to lie); the Martello Tower; in front of the Wentworth Hotel; in front of the town centre; out to sea.

111 people disagreed with the proposal to move the sculpture. Three were emphatic about it in their responses. Comments included: "let it stay", ""looks nice here", "not a problem", "not doing anyone any harm", "OK where it is", "needs a big space", "really good where it is", "an appropriate place", "looks better on the beach", "perfect here", "really good where it is", "brave decision to put it here", "well away from town", "it's OK here", "suits the beach".

27 people said they would like to know more about why there was a local campaign to move the sculpture.

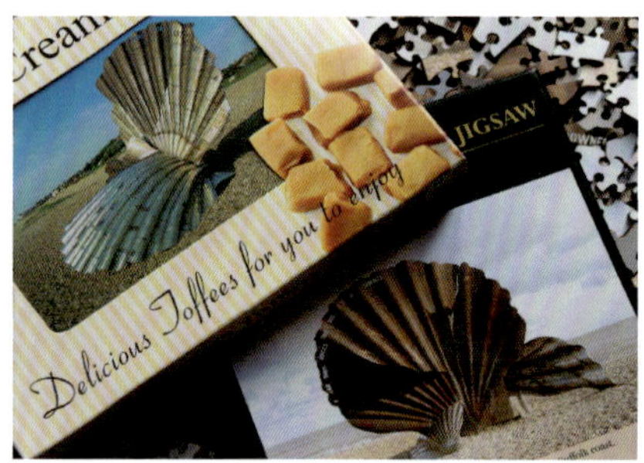

Toffees and jigsaws using images of *Scallop*

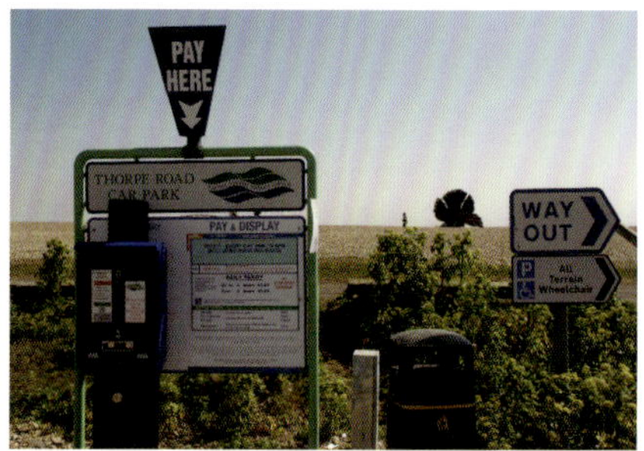

The view from the car park

Sixteen people said they had no opinion about whether it should be moved. Of these, seven said that, as visitors, they felt it would not be appropriate to comment on a local issue.

Where are you from?

Of the total of 193 respondents, 12 were children and 35 had come especially to see the sculpture. Fifteen people came from Aldeburgh, 21 from Ipswich, 14 from Woodbridge. The majority of the rest came from Norfolk, Essex and other parts of Suffolk. The exceptions included 13 people from London, four from Northumberland, six from Buckinghamshire, four from Wiltshire, two from Edinburgh, one from Kent, one from Italy and one from Houston, Texas, who said he was originally from Suffolk.

Have you come especially to see the sculpture?

Thirty-five people said that they had made a special journey to see the sculpture. These included eight from Ipswich, five from Colchester, four from Bungay, two from Gazeley, two from Felixstowe, two from West Mersea, two from Great Olney in Buckinghamshire, one from Cambridge, one from Grantham, one from Woodbridge and one from Southolt.

Those from more distant places were generally staying locally and had, like most respondents in this category, heard about the sculpture on television or in local newspapers.

One interviewee, from Framlingham, suggested that all the media attention given to the *Scallop* might be a conspiracy by the tourist board to get more people on to the beach in January.

Letter to the Aldeburgh Gazette *12.12.2003*

I am writing in response to the letters in recent Gazettes regarding the *Scallop*. I have to say I found the comments interesting to say the least.

My father and I spent seven months fabricating the sculpture, of which the company is very proud. I am, therefore, extremely disappointed at the reaction it has received from some of your readers. To have it branded 'amateurish' and likened to 'scrap corrugated iron' I find hurtful. People should appreciate the time and experience

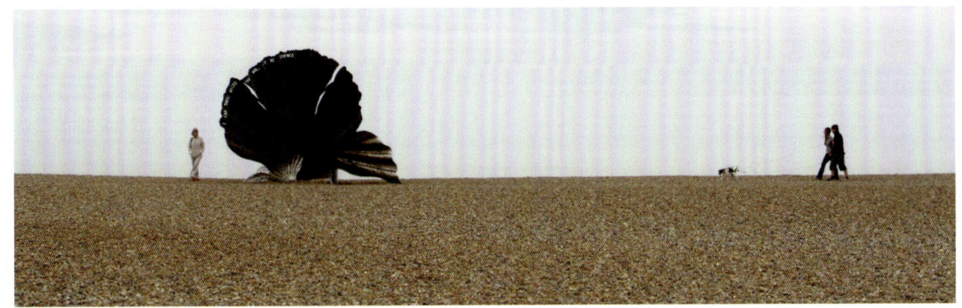

Silhouetted on the shingle

that has gone into making this piece, especially with the difficulties of using stainless steel, and the fact it was manufactured by a company that has been established in the town for just shy of 100 years.

As with any structure a planning application was submitted for approval. This would have appeared in the EADT and been put before the Aldeburgh Town and Parish Councils, giving everyone a chance for comment before the site was finalised. Careful consideration was taken when choosing the site as Benjamin Britten took a lot of inspiration from the sea. Any other position would neither have been relevant or appropriate.

This piece is a credit to Aldeburgh and as such will attract people to the town. This in turn will benefit the local economy through the increased revenue they will bring. Therefore in my opinion all businesses should embrace the sculpture for all the benefits it will produce.

Remember Aldeburgh, this work is a gift from the accredited Maggi Hambling OBE to the town in memory of one of your most gifted residents. On all counts you should be honoured.
Dennis Pegg, J.T.Pegg & Sons Ltd

Roger Hambling
Roger Hambling, MH's brother, told her after overhearing the word "scallop" in a conversation between two drinkers in a Norfolk pub:
"They should've had that there in the war. It would've kept the Germans out and saved on the barbed wire."

A selection of press coverage

SCULPTURE FOR BRITTEN – Council backs plan
(East Anglian Daily Times 11/12/2002)

SCULPTURE SITE DEEMED TOO NEAR TOWN
(EADT 16/04/2003)

SHELL SCULPTURE TAKES SHAPE FOR
BEACHSIDE – Artist begins work despite £30,000
funds shortfall (EADT 06/05/2003)

SPLIT OVER SCULPTURE SCHEME – Council set
to discuss moves for statue to honour composer
(EADT 28/06/2003)

SCULPTURE TO GO ON BEACH – Planners give
go-ahead despite some opposition.
(EADT 24/07/03)

BRITTEN DREAM CLOSER TO A REALITY –
Sculpture taking shape. (EADT 25/08/2003)

A WORD IN YOUR SHELL-LIKE; GET THAT
MONSTROSITY OFF OUR BEACH
(The Guardian 03/11/2003)

SEASHORE SEASHELLS DIVIDE OPINION
(EADT 15/11/2003)

FOUR HUNDRED SIGN PETITION TO MOVE
BRITTEN TRIBUTE FROM BEACH
(EADT 20/12/2003)

LEAVE SCULPTURE WHERE IT IS
(EADT 23/12/2003)

ARTIST SHELLSHOCKED BY SCULPTURE
CRITICS –Petition launched to 'reclaim' beach
(EADT 05/01/2004)

ALDEBURGH WANTS SHOT OF BRITTEN SHELL
(The Guardian 06/01/2004)

VANDALS ATTACK BRITTEN SHELL TRIBUTE
(The Times 21/01/2004)

'YOU DECIDE, LEADER TELLS WARRING TOWN'
(EADT 23/01/2004)

VICTORY FOR SHELL-SHOCKED ALDEBURGH
(The Daily Telegraph 24/01/2004)

CAST VOTE FOR SHELL'S FUTURE – Poll seeks
readers' opinions (EADT 02/02/2004)

SHELL-SHOCKED ALDEBURGH IN TOURIST
BOOM – visitors flock to see sculpture
(EADT 11/02/2004)

SCALLOP MUST STAY! – Readers' overwhelming
verdict in poll (EADT 21/02/2004)

DECISION DRAWS A LINE UNDER SCALLOP
(EADT 20/03/2004)

PROTESTERS LOSE BATTLE OF BRITTEN'S
MONUMENT (The Daily Telegraph 22/03/2004)

NEW THREAT TO SCALLOP – Fresh demands for
relocation (EADT 09/06/2004)

SCALLOP CAMPAIGNER SAYS FIGHT GOES ON
– residents treated with contempt says leader
(EADT 19/06/2004)

IT'S ABOUT TIME TO CLAM UP!
(EADT 29/092004)

SCUPTURE'S FIRST YEAR A STORMY ONE
(EADT 08/11/2004)

THIRD ACT OF VANDALISM ON STEEL
SCULPTURE – Criminal damage is condemned
(EADT 26/11/2004)

CONTROVERSIAL SCALLOP SCOOPS LEADING
AWARD (EADT 25/11/2005)

BATTLE OF BRITTEN RAGES ON THE BEACH
(The Observer 06/01/08)

VOICES OF PROTEST HAVE FINALLY BEEN
DROWNED FOR THE SCALLOP
(EADT 26/04/08)

SCULPTURES I'D LOVE TO SMASH
Charles Spencer (The Daily Telegraph 22.09.2009)

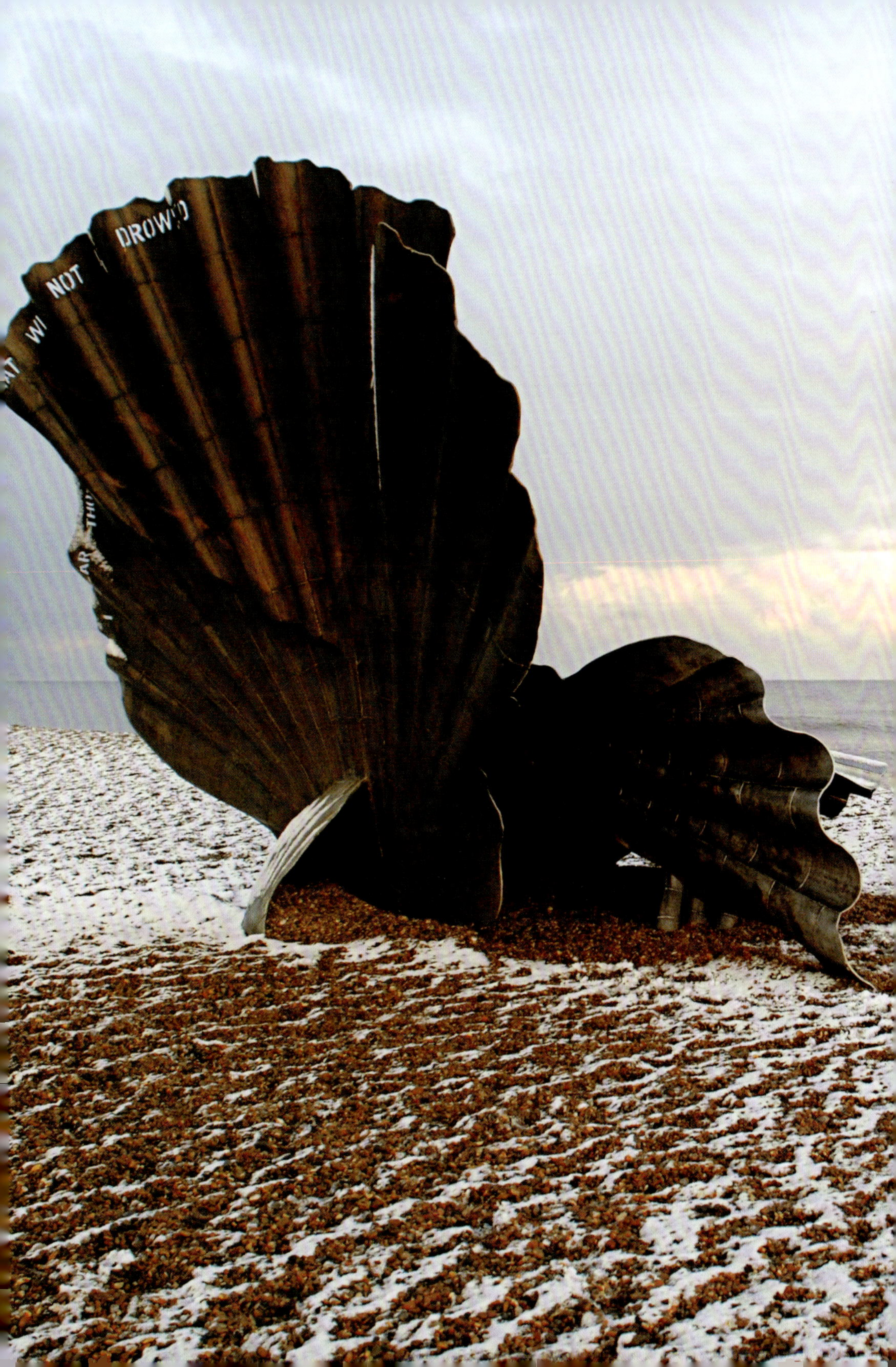
DROW'D
NOT
WI
AT
AR THO

Curriculum vitae

Born   Suffolk 1945

Studied

1960-   With Arthur Lett Haines and Sir Cedric
         Morris, Benton End, Hadleigh, Suffolk
1962-64   Ipswich School of Art
1964-67   Camberwell School of Art
1967-69   Slade School of Fine Art

Awards

1969   Boise Travel Award, New York
1977   Arts Council Award
1980-81   First Artist in Residence,
         National Gallery, London
1995   Jerwood Painting Prize (with Patrick Caulfield)
         Created OBE
2005   Marsh Award for Excellence in Public
         Sculpture for *Scallop*
2010   Created CBE

Exhibitions

1967   *Paintings and Drawings,* Hadleigh Gallery,
         Suffolk
1973   *Paintings and Drawings,* Morley Gallery,
         London
1977   *New Oil Paintings,* Warehouse Gallery,
         London
1981   *Drawings and Paintings on View*
         National Gallery, London
1983   *Pictures of Max Wall,* National Portrait
         Gallery, London and tour

1987   *Maggi Hambling*
         Serpentine Gallery, London
1988   *Moments of the Sun*
         Arnolfini, Bristol and tour
1991   *An Eye Through a Decade,* Yale Center for
         British Art, Newhaven, Connecticut
1992   *The Jemma Series,* monotypes
         Bernard Jacobson Gallery, London
1993   *Dragon Morning,* works in clay
         CCA Galleries, London
1993-4   *Towards Laughter, Maggi Hambling,*
         Northern Centre for Contemporary Art,
         Sunderland, and tour
1996   *Sculpture in Bronze*
         Marlborough Fine Art, London
1997   *A Matter of Life and Death*
         Bothy Gallery, Yorkshire Sculpture Park,
         Wakefield, West Yorkshire
         A conversation with Oscar Wilde
         unveiled Adelaide Street, London, facing
         Charing Cross Station
2000   *Good Friday*
         Gainsborough's House, Sudbury, Suffolk
2001   *Henrietta Moraes* by Maggi Hambling,
         Marlborough Fine Art, London
         Father, Morley College Gallery, London
2003   *The Very Special Brew Series*
         Sotheby's, London
         North Sea Paintings, Snape Maltings
         Concert Hall Gallery, Suffolk
         Scallop, a sculpture to celebrate Benjamin
         Britten, unveiled Aldeburgh, Suffolk

2006 *Portraits of People and the Sea*
Marlborough Fine Art, London
2007 *No Straight Lines*, Octagon Gallery,
Fitzwilliam Museum, Cambridge; Victoria
Art Gallery, Bath; Abbot Hall, Kendall
Waves and Waterfalls, Abbot Hall, Kendall
2008 *Waves and Waterfalls*
Marlborough Fine Art, London
2009 *George Always - Portraits of George Melly by Maggi Hambling*
Walker Art Gallery, Liverpool
National Portrait Gallery, London
The Sea - Paintings by L S Lowry and Maggi Hambling, The Lowry, Salford, Manchster
2010 *Maggi Hambling - The Wave*
Fitzwilliam Museum, Cambridge
New Sea Sculpture
Marlborough Fine Art, London

Books

2001 John Berger, *Maggi and Henrietta: Drawings of Henrietta Moraes by Maggi Hambling*, Bloomsbury, London
Father, facsimile of a sketchbook in the British Museum, Morley Gallery, London
2006 *MAGGI HAMBLING - THE WORKS and conversations with Andrew Lambirth,* Unicorn Press
2009 *George always,* Walker Art Gallery
You are the sea, Lux Books, Suffolk
The Sea, Lowry Press, Salford

Selected Public Collections

Arts Council, England
Ashmolean Museum, Oxford
Australian National Gallery, Canberra
Birmingham City Art Gallery
British Council
British Museum
Contemporary Art Society
Fitzwilliam Museum, Cambridge
Government Art Collection
Gulbenkian Foundation, Lisbon
Imperial War Museum, London
Jerwood Foundation
National Gallery, London
National Portrait Gallery, London
Scottish National Gallery of Modern Art, Edinburgh
Scottish National Portrait Gallery, Edinburgh
Southampton Art Gallery
Tate Collection
Victoria & Albert Museum, London
Wakefield Art Gallery
Whitworth Art Gallery, Manchester
Yale Center for British Art, Newhaven, Connecticut

Acknowledgements

I would like to thank the marvellously patient Louis Baum for his 'tinkering', without which my words would have meandered all over the place.

The photograph on page 2 is by the artist Chris Newson. He came into my life in 2008 and we worked together to produce his DVD film *Storm*. This work combines *Scallop*, Britten's music and me drawing the sea. Chris Newson now cares for the sculpture by shovelling shingle back into place after children have dug down to try to discover how she rises from below ground.

All paintings and drawings by Maggi Hambling unless otherwise stated.

Drawings on pages 70-71 © Jason Gathorne-Hardy 2003
Text on page 12 from the libretto to Benjamin Britten's *Peter Grimes* by Montagu Slater
Thanks to *Private Eye* for permission to reprint *An Aldeburgh Taxi Driver Writes* p.86
Big sea, (p.24-5) reproduced by permission, Norfolk Museums and Archaeology Service

The photographs are by:
Douglas Atfield, p.60
John Christie, p.6, p.14, p.16, p.18, p.42, p.54, p.58, p.64(l), p.75(r), p.77, p.78, p.79, p.81
David Godbold, p.37, p.41
Simon Loftus, p.44, p.48, p.52, p.72(l)
Eamonn McCabe, p.50, p.62, p.75(l)
Claire and Dennis Pegg, p.46, p.47, p.65, p.66, p.67, p.68, p.69, p.72(r), p.74, p.85
Miki Slingsby, p.21, p.23, p.24, p.27

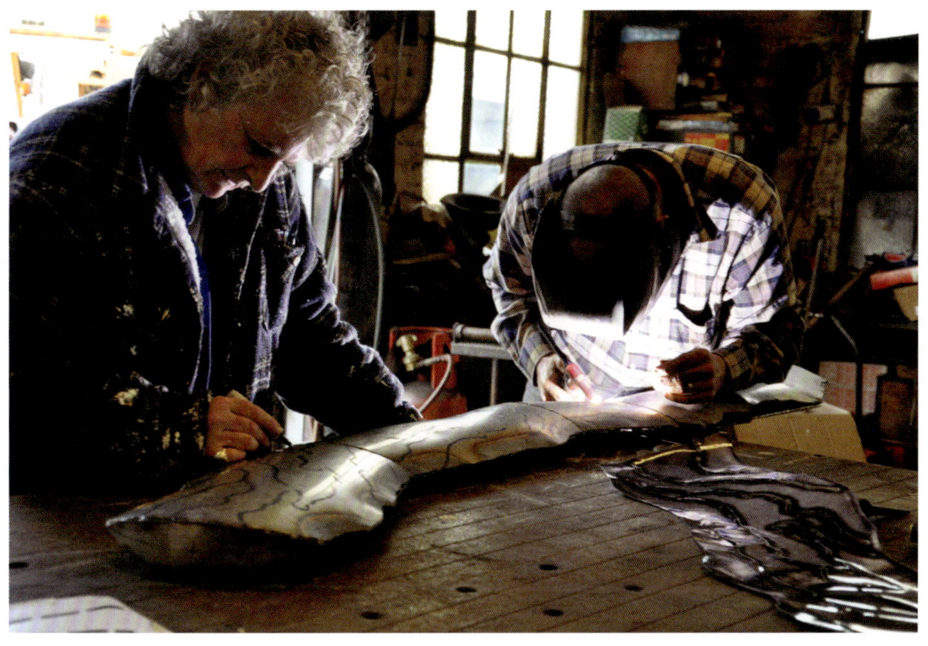

MH and Dennis Pegg at work on *The Brixton Heron,* June 2010

Private Eye '6.2.04. 23

An Aldeburgh Taxi Driver Writes

Every week a well-known taxi driver discusses an issue of topical importance.

THIS WEEK: **Simon Bentley-Marchant,** proprietor of the Peter Pears Limousine Hire Co, Aldeburgh, Suffolk (Cab No. 1), gives his views on the new memorial sculpture to the late Benjamin Britten by Maggie Hambling, recently unveiled on Aldeburgh beach.

"I say, guvnor, that sculpture really is a bit of a shocker. Completely ruins the shoreline. I've got nothing against Ben Britten personally, but what's this shell got to do with anything? Don't get me wrong, it's not because, you know, he played for the other side, if you get my drift, and had a rather poor war, running off to America like that as soon as the first shot was fired, not to mention the fact that his music was, let's face it, unlistenable to, dreary operas about paedophiles and so on, no, it's the council I blame for allowing them to put up a thing like that in the first place. If you ask me, they should all be strung up, it's the only language they understand. I had that Maggie Hambling in the back of the limo once and I asked her not to smoke, 'f*** off' she said, that's the sort of people we get in Aldeburgh nowadays."

First published in 2010 by Full Circle Editions
This paperback edition first published in 2013

Parham House Barn, Brick Lane, Framlingham, Woodbridge, Suffolk IP13 9LQ
www.fullcircle–editions.co.uk

Set in Palatino Light & Gill Sans
Printed on 150gsm GPrint Matt from FSC® Mix Credit

Book design: Jonathan Christie

Printed and bound in Suffolk by Healeys Print Group, Ipswich

ISBN 978-0-9571528-3-0

Note on the typeface:
Hermann Zapf's *Palatino*—designed for the Stempel foundry in 1950—takes its inspiration
from printing types cut by Francesco Griffo (c. 1495) in the print shop of Aldus Manutius,
and is one of the most widely used typefaces in the world today. Named after the 16th
century Italian master of calligraphy, Giambattista Palatino, *Palatino* is based on the
humanist fonts of the Italian Renaissance, which mirror the letters formed by a broad nib
pen. Although Zapf originally intended it to be a display face, its grace and legibility make it
a frequent choice for setting text.

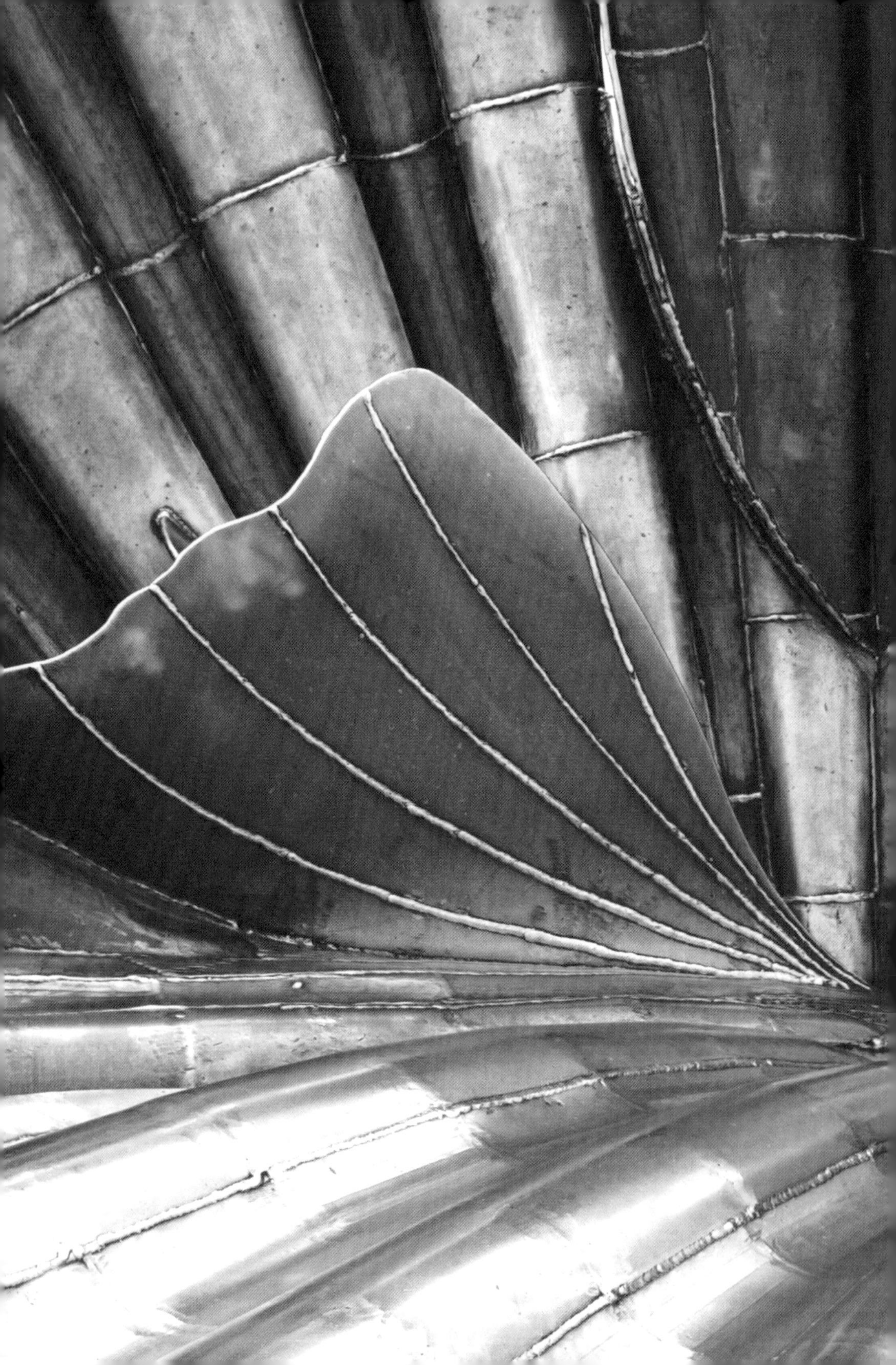